A TRUE STORY

SHOULD'VE BEEN DEAD

LESSONS FROM A CRACK ADDICT
WHO BROKE FREE

SWETA PATEL
WITH RORY LONDER

Cover and design by David Prendergast
Edited by Carmen Riot Smith and Anna Krusinski
Author photos by Erin Sinnwell

First Edition

Published by BookSplash Publishing LLC
Rochester, Minnesota
http://booksplashpublishing.com

Publisher's Cataloging-in-Publication data
Names: Patel, Sweta, author. | Londer, Rory, author.
Title: Should've been dead : lessons from a crack addict who broke free / Sweta Patel with Rory Londer. Description: Includes bibliographical references. | Rochester, MN: Booksplash Publishing, 2023.

Identifiers: LCCN: 2023921048 | ISBN: 979-8-9891700-1-2 (hardcover) | 979-8-9891700-0-5 (paperback) | 979-8-9891700-2-9 (e-book)

Subjects: LCSH Londer, Rory. | Drug addicts--Biography. | Substance abuse--Patients--Biography. | Recovering addicts--Biography. | Businessmen--Biography. | Conduct of life. | Self-actualization (Psychology) | BISAC BIOGRAPHY & AUTOBIOGRAPHY / Memoirs | SELF-HELP / Substance Abuse & Addictions / Drugs Classification: LCC HV5805.L66 P38 2023 | DDC 362.29092--dc23

WHAT READERS ARE SAYING

I found myself cheering for Rory as I learned to know and love him through his struggles and triumphs. There is an honesty and authenticity in his words and his journey that have stayed with me long after reading his story.

    - Heather Willman, Director of Academics (Secondary)

I could empathize with the broken, struggling human being and his feelings of failure. He fell short, faced overwhelming odds, and was exhausted from fighting uphill for so long. His pain was evident. I felt the pull of addiction. The hopelessness of escape. The danger of being drawn back in.

    - Jay Wangen, Bank Vice President

This story is real, raw, and painful, but throughout it all, his love of life and determination to leave a positive mark in the community persevered. Rory's story is an example of how, at any point, we each have the power to say, "This is not how the story ends." Truly inspirational.

    - Leah Baethke, High School English Teacher

It's beautiful. It's true. It's honest. It's brave… and not just Rory's story, but Sweta's too. A blossoming friendship. You've bared your hearts and souls and shown your love for the world, sharing it with whoever is open to hearing it. That is this book, one that I desperately needed. I am changed. Thank you! Thank you! Thank you!

- Julie Ruzek, Executive Director, Cradle2Career

A real page-turner, I wanted to find out how Rory's journey would unfold. But I also loved hearing how the author applied Rory's lessons in her personal and teaching life. I applaud Sweta for not only trusting her instinct in writing the book, but also her perseverance and discipline in making it happen. I can't wait for the next one!

- Alexis Zaccariello, High School Art Teacher

I finished this book in one day. It's written from the heart, as real as can be. I saw myself in Rory's story and had to know how things ended. There's hope for all of us.

- Inga, Mentor to those in recovery

DEDICATION

To those who are hopeless, suffering, living in fear,
or feeling alone—things can change. - R.L.

To RALC students—past, present, and future.
And to Rory—your life continues to give, and give,
and give. - S.P.

NOTE TO THE READER

For privacy, names and identifying details have been changed unless permission was granted. During my interviews with Rory's close family and friends, they sometimes shared thoughts, feelings, and life events that Rory may or may not have been aware of. To maintain a smooth narrative flow, I chose to have these secondary characters reveal those details to Rory. Given Rory's history of drug use and chemotherapy, the exact timeline of events is sometimes blurry for him. This book is an honest representation of our lives from our current recollections. Finally, Alcoholics Anonymous encourages anonymity so no one person comes before the message. We don't claim to represent the organization in any way or to criticize alternative approaches to recovery. Rory and a few other members have chosen to identify themselves and to share their story with you to raise awareness around addiction and inspire hope.

CONTENTS

INTRODUCTION

"Just to warn you, he swears. A lot." I prepped my high school class for tomorrow's speaker.

"His name is Rory Londer. He had a crack addiction, was living on the streets, and ended up buying the same laundromat he used to rest in. He turned the place into a million-dollar home improvement business."

"What?!! No way! How'd he do that?"

"You'll have to wait for his answer."

Five years ago, Rory spoke to my students at the Alternative Learning Center in Rochester, Minnesota, for the first time. To enroll at the ALC, ninth- through twelfth-grade students have to meet at least one of the following criteria:

- perform substantially below grade level
- be behind in credits for graduation
- be pregnant or parenting
- have experienced physical or sexual abuse
- be chemically dependent
- have mental health problems

- have been homeless recently
- have withdrawn from school or been chronically truant
- speak English as a second language or have limited English proficiency

I often invite motivational speakers into my College Success class. Our school intentionally offers a section because so few of our students opt for post-secondary enrollment options, where they can enroll in classes at the local community college for free while still in high school. I needed to develop their inner belief that they *can* have goals past high school, and they *can* go on to further education if those goals require it. Week after week, with each new class, the students and I get to know each other through regular journal writing. I read their entries, sometimes blinking back tears, and mentally stagger at just how deep their wounds run.

A student shared that her parents were in Mexico and she was living here with her uncle. At home, she frequently heard she was worthless, lazy, and incapable. Another wrote of transferring to the ALC when he was caught selling weed at his home high school. He was kicked off the hockey team—his mental health lifeline—and was angry at the world. Another spoke of his freshman year when his dad was in a coma and he had to help his mom decide whether to pull the plug or not. He'd been withdrawn and numb ever since. I read stories of addiction, toxic relationships, foster homes, bullying, depression, suicide attempts, anxiety, moving around... They all had one thing in common: a world of hurt. Life after graduation was the last thought on their minds. They were just trying to make it through the day.

Throughout the year, I take recommendations from colleagues and bring in speakers from the community to help my students get unstuck, even the tiniest nudge forward, and open a new way of thinking about themselves and who they want to be. When the speaker finishes, I ask my students to write letters to them to share any connections or takeaways. Usually, they write for about five minutes, politely stack their papers, and pack up their bags.

With Rory, it's different. He has a presence. He walks in wearing a black, tattered *Rory's Home Improvement* hoodie with white paint stains. He's a little over fifty, stands at five foot nine with a small frame of one hundred and fifty pounds. When he's ready to start, he gives his shaved head a couple of nervous pats, slides into an armchair at the front of the classroom, and gets down to the students' level.

"I'm here to tell you my story," he begins, "and it's a fucking good one." He looks straight at them, holding his gaze with as many souls as he can. When he continues, he moves his whole body while talking a mile a minute. It's never scripted as he trusts the memories will come in the order he needs them for the audience in front of him. A different compilation of snapshots always leads to the same message: he made it, and you can too.

When Rory's talk ends, I smile as I look around the room. Heads bent down over loose-leaf paper, a rush of writing. I finally call time so they won't be late for their next class. There's something special here, I can feel it—a strong pull between speaker and audience.

In 2020, with the looming threat of the coronavirus, we moved to distance learning where I taught from home. That winter, I emailed Rory asking if he would be willing to be a virtual class speaker. A few days later, I received a gut-wrenching response from his assistant: Rory was diagnosed with stage IV lung cancer. He had good days and bad, and right now, it was a bad day. The words blurred heavy across the screen. I was devastated.

I sank back into my chair and thought of Rory sitting on my classroom floor with his knees tucked close to his chest as he spoke. *If I was lucky, someone would have just run a dryer, and I could scoot up to it like this to stay warm.* Then he would slowly stand, pointing to the imaginary laundromat and say: *I own that now. It's my office. And every time I pass that spot, I remember where I came from.* One day at a time, he'd made it.

But now this. How could a person bear much more? I sent Rory a message of gratitude for sharing his time with our students over the years. I was glad to hear he was slowly improving and managing his pain.

I made it through the school year despite wave after wave of new COVID-19 protocols, even teaching students quarantined at home and in the classroom simultaneously. Outside of school, I was managing my kid's tantrums in the toy aisle over a Hot Wheels car he just had to have. I was ready for an outlet.

That summer of 2021, I saw a group running laps outside of Burn Boot Camp, a local gym. I felt a pull, but with a rush of self-doubt. Growing up, I groaned every time the P.E. teacher assigned two captains to form teams. I knew I'd be the last kid picked. I was clumsy and couldn't run or catch a ball. These formative experiences shaped my thoughts about what I was physically capable of…which wasn't much. But now, desperate for time to work on myself, I signed up.

When I looked around that gym, people could lift heavier weights, jump squat, and hold perfect form. And there I was, bent over and gasping. A few months in—and I'll never forget this day—one of the stations involved jumping onto a twenty-inch black box. The modification was to step up and down, and that's what I did without a second thought. After a few minutes, the trainer came over and asked if I'd like to attempt the jump. My answer was instinctual: *I can't.*

He kneeled beside the box and gently encouraged, "I'll be right here. You can do hard things. I'll catch you if you fall." There was no time to think. I took a deep breath, silenced the negative noise in my head, and jumped. My feet hit the edge and I fell backward, but he steadied me. I could hear sympathetic recognition all around me. "Go again," he said. "Focus on bringing your knees up high. Swing your arms up for power. You can do it." He didn't know that decades of negative self-talk were flowing through me, that his words were helping to rewrite mine. I stared at the box for half a minute, trying to build up courage. I swung my arms and jumped with all I had in me. I landed it to claps and cheers.

Maybe it was how the trainer's voice in my ear reminded me of Rory's as he jolted my students out of thinking they'd never be able to move on from their situations. Or maybe I was riding the high of being capable of more than I ever thought. But that night, I voiced to my husband what had been rolling around in my head for a while: *I think I'm supposed to write Rory's story.* I told him about Rory, how he had changed course in life, and about his cancer. I had no professional writing experience, yet there was something compelling me to do this before it was too late. Sharing the idea aloud scared me. I sat in uncertainty till I repeated *you can do hard things* long enough to email Rory at the start of the new school year: *One, can we set a date for you to speak to my class, and two, I think I'm supposed to write your story.* I received a reply soon after: *Yes and yes—I think it's time.*

We started meeting on Saturday mornings at his home improvement business. His memories came flooding back, and I listened from the perspective of an ALC student and a teacher. We met for months, and soon, I had over a hundred pages of shorthand notes and many hours of video footage, not just from Rory. I had the opportunity to interview those in his inner circle as well—his wife, daughter, brother, friends, and former sponsees.

With young kids at home, it was difficult to carve out time to craft these notes into a motivational book, so I took a chance. I applied for a sabbatical leave for the 2022-2023 school year, and it was granted. The sabbatical committee, the superintendent, and the school board recognized the impact Rory's story might have on others. I hope that impact continues to go something like this[1]:

Student Letter #1: *"Rory, you're a reminder that it doesn't matter if others say I'm not going anywhere in life. What matters is what I believe. Not many people try to see me at eye level, so they don't know what it feels like to struggle. I know a lot of people wouldn't be able to do what I do for myself and my family while going to school and working at the same time. I needed to hear that my struggles are actually a sign of my strength…and to try to snap out of the negative mindset that I've always had."* - Emma

Student Letter #2: *"I connected with how you were exposed to horrible things when you were younger. I struggle with addictions and past trauma, and you showed me that I don't have to be stuck in this place forever. No matter where I come from, I can always better myself. And even though you were going through a hard time, you'd think of others and how to help them, and that helped you too. I want that."* - Mario

----

[1] Reprinted with permission. Names have been changed.

Student Letter #3: *"My mom has an extreme alcohol addiction, and I've been feeling suicidal. You told us that we could do whatever we wanted, that we don't have to be our parents, that we can write our own story. It made me believe in myself again and to feel less alone."* - Angie

Student Letter #4: *"I've always struggled with school. So when I pictured myself working with animals, maybe as a vet tech, I'd erase it from my mind as quick as it came. I'm working at a Kwik Trip gas station right now and figured it's what I'll keep doing. But hearing your story of how you'd sleep on the streets to owning your own business was like opening a door I didn't know existed. I'm still scared of my future, and just talking about it makes my stomach turn, but I want to start putting myself out there now."* - Grace

To anyone crushed in the quicksand of *I'm a failure, I'm lost, I'm a bad person, I'm defective, I'm unlovable...I can't, I won't, I'll never*—I hope this collection of learned truths from Rory's life moves you to try, not just to exist but *to live*.

When the book begins, we follow Rory in his addiction till he's bent over with the weight of his failure. Though he couldn't see it at the time, these experiences led to the twelve hard-earned life lessons that followed. Through each, he slowly recovered the belief that he mattered. Each lesson title is a phrase from Rory's story, one that comes up most often as I go about my day—simple but so impactful in forcing me to pause and carefully consider what I'll say or do next. That is Rory's legacy: to inspire, to lift, to change, to move.

I will ask of you what I ask of my students: When you hear his story, what connections can you make? What are your takeaways?

What does it move you to change in your life? The reflection questions in the appendix encourage an even deeper dive into Rory's story and ourselves.

When Rory first shared that he often thought of writing a book from his experiences, I asked him why he hadn't yet. *Sweta, I can't focus on one thing for more than two minutes. And imagine a Canadian goose pecking at the ground? Well, that's me on a keyboard with two fingers. With stage IV lung cancer, I don't know that I've got the time for that.* So he let me. Together, we connected the dots from his past to present and brought new meaning to his experiences. I've purposely chosen to tell Rory's story in *his voice* so readers can sit with him, eye to eye. I want you to listen, laugh, and cry with him, just as my students and I have.

Where Rory's story ends, mine begins. When I started this project, I intended to simply record his memories. My first outline was strictly chronological. It was both an addiction/recovery story and a rags-to-riches tale. But, over the course of our interviews, I knew his story had even more to give. I began practicing his messages, and something magical happened: I gained confidence. My relationships with students and in my personal life deepened into meaningful, authentic connections. In fact, with Rory's voice in my ear, I had the best interactions with students in my fifteen years of teaching. In the afterword, I chronicle these transformative moments—moments when I felt genuine, present (and not living in my head), and ready to say *yes* to life. His lessons aren't for the addict alone.

(Photo Credit: Erin Sinnwell Photography)

NOTE FROM RORY

Yes, I swear. A lot. When I'm telling my story, it's almost like I'm back there again on the streets of Minneapolis. Some have even said my voice drops and I become who I was—"Hey, motherfucka, what up?" And if I have to change out words where I'm not swearing, then I'm changing my story.

I've spoken in schools, churches, treatment centers, recovery meetings, and in front of hundreds of people at an AA convention. I used to hide my past, but today, I don't care anymore. I want everyone to know. People tell me I can bring them to tears to laughter to inspiration in a matter of an hour by just telling my story. I was ashamed for so long. To know now that my life brings hope is a gift.

With stage IV lung cancer, I don't know how much time I have left—maybe a year, maybe another twenty. What better way is there to spend my time? I joke about driving my dream car. But I don't really need anything. I can live pretty simply with a backpack and some change. I want to keep making an impression on people and leaving an effect. I can't make a better mark on this world than that.

Now, hang on for the ride. It's called *My Life*.

(Photo Credit: Erin Sinnwell Photography)

MOMENT OF CRISIS

In 2001, thirteen years after my first hit of crack cocaine, I finished treatment at the Pathway House. Within months, I was pounding down Bacardi Cokes and hunting for dope in dark alleys again. I wandered through downtown Rochester, Minnesota, into a SuperAmerica gas station one cold night, craving cigarettes.

An eighteen-year-old, who looked stoned, was working the counter. "Hey, man..."

Seeing an opportunity, I leaned in close, locked eyes with the guy, and pitched him an offer. "Dude, hey. Give me the dough from the till. Come on, man, let's make a deal. I'll put half of it in your hubcap. That sweet ride out there is yours, right? Just take off and whatever, man."

With a mix of fear and doubt, he shook his head. "No, man, I can't. I'm already in trouble. My buddies come here all the time, stealing shit. The owner's got his eyes on me."

As he opened the cash register to count out my change for the smokes, my eyes froze on the stacks of cash just sitting there. Fuck. I wanted that. I followed a pair of bright headlights through the window as a car pulled up to a gas pump. The guy got out, took a drag of his cigarette, and left.

In the next second, I had my hand under my hoodie in the shape of a gun. "Alright, I'm not fucking around. Give me the fucking money, dude. I'm not playing."

"Okay, okay, dude. Chill out, man. Relax. Here." He nervously grabbed the money from the register and tossed it in front of me. Then he turned around and opened a secret drawer with a second till I didn't even know about! I gathered the cash, snatched a couple of extra cigarette cartons, and stuffed it all into a plastic bag. An easy four hundred bucks, just like that.

As addicted as I was, I stopped to pick up a twenty rock—twenty dollars worth of crack—and a bottle of Bacardi before checking into a second-floor room at a cheap motel. I filled the ice bucket, then let the door slam shut, got high, and poured myself a cold, smooth drink. When I turned on the TV and flipped through the channels, I froze. There, on the screen, was my face. I turned up the volume and caught some of the description: "Rory Londer, Olmsted County's Most Wanted Man. Born in Saint Louis Park. He's wearing a…" SuperAmerica had six cameras; six different angles caught the whole story on tape.

I'd spent so much of my life high on crack, paranoid that "they" were coming for me. Now, for the first time, they really were. It was yet another moment of crisis where I thought: *I don't know what I want, but I know it isn't this.*

***

Nowadays, when people hear my name, they think of Rory's Home Improvement, my volunteer work in the community, and my beautiful wife, Lilly. When they learn about my crackhead past, they sometimes try to solve my life like a logic puzzle, but my answers only puzzle them more:

No. I grew up with loving parents.

No. I was always good at school. In Hebrew school, too. In fact, I was an honors student.

No. I had dreams. I was an up-and-coming chef at a high-end restaurant.

They pause before asking, "So how does that even happen?"

And I tell them.

FALLING IN LOVE

When Mom met Dad, she already had two young boys. Dad made a promise to adopt them, but on one condition: Mom had to convert to Judaism and have two Jewish boys of their own. She agreed to the arrangement, and when Dad smashed glass under his feet, shouting "L'Chaim! (To Life!)," they were married.

Shortly after, David was born, and a year later, they had me. November 16, 1970, in Saint Louis Park, Minnesota. Mom named me after Rory Calhoun, a cowboy on the big screen who she thought was just so handsome.

They divorced when I turned three. When Dad complained, "Your mom was always looking some other way," Mom would counter, "Your dad was so boring. He wasn't no angel, either, with his pills." I asked him about the little reds years later (which turned out to be speed) and he had no comment.

My dad—Raymond—was an introvert who lived a quiet life in his apartment, alone. Every morning, before work, he would drive to the corner diner for breakfast, order bacon and eggs, and nod to the waitress on his way out. Always the same restaurant, the same booth, the same meal, the same tip. Later, when he retired, the rest of his day was TV and football games. For a change, he'd dust off his stamp collection and mail out a few to auctions and wait for a bid.

My mom—Arnell—was gorgeous, with wild, flowing blond hair and a loud "look at me" personality that couldn't be tamed. Complete with a glittering, sequin dress and a fur coat. She was a model in her day and waitressed at the Pink Pussycat saloon. When she strutted into the room with tight shorts and a bunny tail, heads would turn. Men's heads. Whatever she said, they listened with a "yes, ma'am" and would fall back into their seats with wide eyes. She'd shake her tail and collect tips. Her drink of choice was a mimosa, and on some days, she had a glass in her hand by 10 a.m.—a sweet, golden-yellow blend of champagne and orange juice.

When Dad walked into the Pink Pussycat one evening, Mom must have seen security and stability. At the time, he was managing his family's upholstery company and was under pressure to start a family of his own. They struck their deal and got married. But for Mom, without love, it fell apart.

I was too young to hold on to any pain or resentment over the divorce. I grew up with a "weekend dad" who had it easy. He'd honk twice on Sunday mornings and drive us straight to a trout farm with a restaurant that would cook up whatever we caught. Other times, we would go to the movies, visit the zoo, explore museums, or just drive around the airport to watch planes taking off. On Yom Kippur, Purim, and Rosh Hashana, we went to the synagogue and gathered around kosher dishes with our aunts and uncles. During Hanukkah, Dad always surprised my cousins and me with gifts from Radio Shack—something we had to build or put together.

In the evenings, Dad would take us out to Ember's restaurant for dinner and hand over a clipped coupon from the paper for free dessert. Dad wasn't a hugger, but every so often, he'd give us a quick kiss on the cheek. He loved all four sons the same and never yelled at us, not even when we'd wrestle each other into a headlock and accidentally break something. At the end of the night, he'd drive us back home to Mom.

Every year on our birthdays, Mom had this tradition of making a reservation for two at a Japanese steakhouse. We'd sit at the tableside grill as the chef sautéed noodles, meats, and rice, and Mom would sneak us a taste of her warm sake. She'd joke till her laughs became howls, even drawing in the other diners. On nights when we tossed and turned with high fevers and coughing fits, Mom would take out her trusty Vicks VapoRub and smear it on our chests. She had an oversized, fluffy green robe that she would wrap around us. It became the "sick robe." She'd even put a bell beside our beds so we could call her if we needed anything. But if we happened to hear Mom cough twice or even hint at feeling under the weather, my brothers and I would look at each other with panic in our eyes and run through the house till we found that bell and had it securely hidden away. Otherwise, we would hear our names, from oldest to youngest, over and over with a "Bring me some soup!" or, "I need some tea!" or, "Make me this… Rory?!" *Ringgggg!* She enjoyed it too much. If she was too sick to get out of bed, she'd send us to the local drugstore with cash and notes: "Please sell my son cough medicine and one pack of cigarettes." Later, David and I would forge these notes and keep the cigarettes for ourselves.

Whenever Mom could get away, we'd go up to her cabin on Mille Lacs Lake, where she would relax, smoke, drink, and giggle on the phone with the different men who revolved in and out of our lives. Meanwhile, we boys would chase each other through rows of raspberry bushes and sprint toward Grandpa's place for a day of fishing. Sitting by the lake with him or watching him garden felt safe. He was never angry or lifted a hand or raised his voice.

One lazy Saturday morning, David and I were playing with our BB guns when we accidentally shot a robin. We had taken aim, believing we would miss or it would fly away as birds usually do. When Grandpa came running out and caught sight of the dead bird, we made ourselves look at him and it wrecked us to see his tears. "You don't kill something unless it's to eat. You don't just kill it." We cherished him—he was so pure—and his disappointment gutted us.

Dad always hoped one of his sons would graduate from Talmud Torah, a Jewish school in Minneapolis. The synagogue awarded a grant when he couldn't afford the tuition, and I learned to speak, read, and write Hebrew after school from sixth to ninth grade. Later, in jail, other inmates would seek me out—"Rory the Jew"—to translate Hebrew passages from the Torah. I'd sit in the courtyard with these big honchos, huddled together over scriptures. I was useful, and under their protection, I'd be left alone.

As the youngest of four boys, deep down, I always felt less than, smaller than, less intelligent, less capable. We fought all the time—shoving, kicking, elbowing—and then limped around with scabs crusted over our lips. Mom could never go to the grocery store and pick up a few things, get in and out. We'd barrel through the aisles, knocking boxes out of each other's hands. I can't think of a single time when my brothers and I hugged.

At home, there was a revolving door of babysitters as my brothers would flush their cigarettes down the toilet and relentlessly ridicule them, especially Mrs. Friedman, who smelled like the guppies in her fish tank. One night, my brother, Tim, coaxed me inside a dog kennel and locked the cage and bathroom door behind him. When she heard me crying, she gently instructed me to open the door. I cried back, "I can't. I can't!" "You see?" I heard my brother say. "I told you he's slow. He just won't do it." When she finally unlocked the door and found me curled up, gripping the cage bars, and crying hysterically, we never saw her again.

When my stronger and faster brothers were rough with me, as brothers are, I had to fight back harder. If we'd drive toward Porky's near Lake Calhoun for a bite to eat and they'd sneer, "Hey, Rory, we're going to *your* place!" I'd shout back an insult. They made me competitive, and that affected my character. I had a drive to survive and come out on top. So the more Mrs. Blackman, my Torah teacher, showered me with, "Oh, Rory! You're our best student here!" the more I worked for her praise. She'd snap at the other kids when she caught them passing notes or talking during her lesson, but she loved me. I was the first to raise my hand to answer her questions and the first to deliver my test to her desk. I always made the Honor Roll list. At home, Mom would compliment me with, "Why can't your brothers be more like you?" while she chided them, "Rory does so well. He's the only good son around here."

As a kid, I'd lose track of time poring through *Popular Mechanics* magazines at school; it's where my love of building things with my own two hands started. I built a tree fort on stilts with a deck, and later, a wooden go-kart. When I'd shove off downhill, the wheels would break and I'd spin out. I reconstructed it over and over to keep the wheels on but couldn't do it. The train set I built worked better. I set up a track and trains and little people on fake grass across plywood in the garage, and even engineered a pulley system. I'd tug on a rope to lift the board up when Mom needed to park her car. Every so often, I'd sneak a few twenties out of Mom's rent pouch and walk to the toy store at Ridgedale Mall. I'd buy new pieces to add to my collection, maybe a mail station with a man whose arms would move up and down. When Mom eventually caught me, she threatened to send me to the army.

In all the years I spent rocking back and forth reciting Hebrew prayers and working on my trains till late at night, my classmates were busy playing spin the bottle and kissing girls. But now, I'd finally graduated from Talmud Torah and was getting ready to start tenth grade. I had a chance to see what I'd been missing out on, only to watch my family running in and out with their own places to go. While Mom got dolled up for another party, Tim would leave to go clubbing just as David's friends were piling in. I was tired of sitting on the couch alone, so when David got his driver's license, I asked to tag along.

He and his older friends smoked pot in his run-down yellow Malibu, and to fit in, I did too. Each time, I felt a sense of calm wash through me, and we would giggle through a cloud of smoke. We fed our munchies with a round of nachos and drowned our cottonmouth with a Tahitian Treat Fruit Punch. Tim snuck us beers, and David and I swiped cigarettes from Mom's stash. We got bolder, and at night, our group would scope out large apartment complexes. We timed it perfectly and stole radios and radar detectors from parked cars. When a trusted friend sold them for us, we used the money to restock our beer and pot.

At home, Tim had boxes of *Playboy* magazines stashed under his mattress. I'd sell them to the nerdy kids at school for three dollars a piece, or ten for any issues with Madonna. Tim would take the cash and throw me some commission. I had a sense for doing business early. Inspired, I bought catnip from the pet store and let it sit with a banana peel. I spread the word to my classmates that I had banana weed for sale. The next day, they caught up to me and bragged, "Dude, that was so good!" I bit my lip to keep from laughing and stuffed their cash into my jeans pocket.

Before summer ended, Mom walked up to David and me and said, "Well, boys, I'm moving to Alabama. It's time for me to go somewhere warmer. You can either come with me or stay here with your dad." My older brothers were adults and chose to stay behind in their own apartments. David and I had hardly lived with Dad, so we followed.

Foley, Alabama, was another planet. In Minnesota, my junior high school was a sprawling brick complex, complete with a fully stocked gym and a competition pool that I used on the swim team. Now I sat in Foley High School, watching a trail of cockroaches along the classroom walls. There was no swim team. The hallways were roofs held together with wobbly metal poles. To get to the Driver's Ed class, we had to cross an alleyway to a run-down house. And people talked funny—"Y'all come back soon now, ya hear?" I wanted to scream, "It's just me! What do you mean 'y'all'? You seeing people or something?!"

I didn't know anyone and felt out of place. Eventually, David and I buddied up with a guy when we caught a whiff of pot reeking from his beaten-up truck that wouldn't start. We gave him a push in the school parking lot and popped the clutch to get it going. In return, he gave us some weed. Smoking and drinking took away the feeling of being different. I could have a bad day, where I didn't like myself, or I didn't like the kids around me, and the weed and alcohol would do their job. Take away all the hurt. Back home, I'd just been given a taste of a life I had liked—a brotherhood—and I missed it. That's when I met the local surfers. They said, "Dude, we hang out and smoke pot every day and a bunch of chicks party with us. You should join."

That same afternoon, I bought a little red Charlie "CB" Baldwin surfboard and learned to swim out and catch a wave. They messed with me like my brothers did and nicknamed me Dory, short for "dumb Rory." I kept trying and eventually impressed them. They said they were going to trip on Friday. When David and I looked at each other, confused, they added, "You know, drop acid." When the day came, we followed them into the woods to a spot called Hell and lit candles. They passed around tabs—tiny squares of paper with drops of LSD on them. I placed one under my tongue and took in the ride. We took turns moving a pen slowly through the air and tracked the streak of color that trailed behind it, mesmerized. Someone said, "Dude, I think it's definitely kicked in." My jaw hurt from laughing so hard at absolutely nothing.

We skipped school and hung out with our surfer buddies for months before Mom found out. "Do you want me to tell your grandpa what you're up to?"

I stuck it out another year, but sitting at a desk, class after class, reviewing material I had learned in Plymouth years ago… I couldn't do it anymore. I broke the news to Mom that I was moving to Jacksonville, Florida, with a surfer buddy, and I assured her I'd enroll in school there. I kept my promise; I just never showed up to any classes. I'd hide out in the rec room, playing ping-pong and pool and making bets. When the school finally caught on, I left.

I dreamed of becoming a professional surfer. My roommate joined the Eastern Surfing Association and we'd stop at regional contests up and down the coast in my '79 Volkswagen van. I had my fifteen minutes of fame when I outscored a sponsored surfer in a warm-up heat. I surfed on a Spectrum Scorcher tri-fin board now, and when the wave curled, you could see its painted orange and red flames. On the other side, I'd written: "Bite Me."

I got a job as a dishwasher and burned through cash for surfing, weed, alcohol, girls, a skateboarding ramp for the backyard, and my newfound love: crack. One night when I left work, I found the closest working girl on the strip and gave my usual line, "Do you know where I can get some coke?" She invited me back to her place, and the next moment altered my entire life.

We were kneeling in front of a cardboard box with a towel draped over it. It was a makeshift table with her tools—spoons and bottles, a mirror, and a pipe. She picked up the largest spoon, and added baking soda, cocaine, and water to it before holding it over a lighter. As she moved the flame back and forth to a slow rhythm, we watched the mixture bubble, and she swirled the sharp end of a paperclip through the sludge till it thickened and came together as crack. I watched her set the rock on a matchbook to dry before breaking off a piece.

Then she placed the crack into a long glass stem with the smallest piece of a steel wool scouring pad already inside. With her head tipped back, she held the stem high and massaged its sides with the flame until the rock melted into the pad, a filter to keep it from being inhaled. When the smoke began pulling through the glass pipe, she brought it to her lips, twisting and turning it between her fingers so perfectly that the crack never burned under the flame. It was a fucking performance.

I'd smoked weed, dropped acid, and snorted coke before. But I had my first time with crack cocaine in this prostitute's house. With my lips around the warm pipe, I tipped my head back like she had, closed my eyes, sucked in deep, and held the smoke in. I tasted sweetness. The moment I blew out, a deep sense of quiet and peace settled through me—a new experience for the boy whose middle-school nickname was Speedy Gonzalez. Now, all I wanted to do was rush her turn along so I could take another hit. I was already thinking: *How can we make more of this? Do I have enough money? Could she get more coke? I've got baking soda and a lighter at home. Can I just make it myself?* My mind was running and calculating. It took just one hit to find the love of my life that I would chase for the next seventeen years.

Just months later, a week after my eighteenth birthday, I was sitting on a gas station curb on Thanksgiving day with my head in my hands. I'd stopped on the way back from the laundromat. A basket of clothes sat on my bike, and I jingled my last bit of change for dinner. As I chewed on a soggy 99-cent turkey sandwich, I thought of Mom and how I missed her. When I called her from the pay phone, I could hear Grandma and Grandpa in the background, cheerfully chatting among the clinking dishes. My family was together.

When they asked, "How are you doing?" I was quick with an "Oh, I'm good, you good? I'm good." It's what I always said when Mom called. The fine Jewish son who would do so well was pedaling down an empty street, sitting alone on a curb, eating expired bread.

The truth was, I wasn't good. *I didn't know what I wanted, but I knew it wasn't this.* I was getting through life, getting by, getting high, and the money had run out. My roommates had stopped paying their share of the rent, so my life had become a series of midnight moves from couch to couch. That's when I moved back home with Mom.

I'm a failure, I'm a failure, I'm a failure…

Arnell (Rory's mom) and Raymond (Rory's dad)

Young Rory

Rory (middle) with his brother David (left) and his mom, Arnell (right)

Rory catches a wave in Jacksonville, Florida

STUCK LIKE CHUCK

Tacky Jack's Tavern & Grill hired me on as a cook. I've always had a lot of energy, rarely stopping to let others get a word in and gesturing wildly when I talk. Cooking was good for me. I got to take orders, chop, heat, and plate—all at the same time.

When I came home from work one day, Mom stopped me at the door. "Rory, what's crack?" she asked. "David said you're smoking crack?" They wanted to know what it was like.

When I had moved back to Alabama, David and I were older and our relationship with Mom changed. We'd have beers with her, and when she'd catch us smoking pot, she would want us to bring a bag of weed home for her too. She'd get cocaine from one of the bartenders at Tacky Jack's, and David and I would stay up late playing drinking games and doing a little coke with her and her friends. When she was hammered, I'd steal a joint from her purse or sometimes David would. Then we'd check with each other to make sure we didn't take one too many and get caught.

As soon as she asked about crack, I grabbed a spoon. Mom and David didn't care for it, but when I took a hit, I got *stuck* as I always do. You see, drinking gets you sloppy and loud. Snorting coke gets you on max energy. But when I smoked crack, I'd take a hit, slowly blow it out, and get quiet. It makes others restless, but not me. Later, on the streets, they would call me White Boy Fred who got "stuck like Chuck." I would get completely still, and then paranoia would set in. Even now, I peered through the window behind Mom, suspicious of every car that rolled by. I'm hardwired to move and talk fast; it makes me wonder if that's why my body is attracted to the effects that crack has on me—the calm, the silence, and the rest it craves.

When Mom moved to Florida for even warmer weather, I rented a three-bedroom trailer in Orange Beach, Alabama, with David. I used part of my paycheck from Tacky Jack's for rent and took the rest with me every week to the small town of Warrington about thirty minutes away. I'd pull up and two brothers would sell me twenty rocks. Once, I drove up and they ripped me right out the van window, dropped me to the ground, kicked me hard, and walked away with my money and radar detector. Bruised and bent over, I drove back home. They could have killed me. But I only stayed away till my pockets were full of cash again. There was nothing I wouldn't go through for another hit. I was just starting to feed my addiction—little by little, on weekends only for now— setting the stage for what was to come.

I was twenty years old, living check to check, barely making the $250 I needed for rent. How many more years would I surf, smoke weed, party every night, and run to Warrington in between, not knowing if I'd get a rock or a black eye? My buddies, who would smoke crack every once in a while, could pass on it with a wave of their hand as being too expensive or too short a high. Even David could save hits of cocaine for another day. Deep down, I knew I was different when I'd craft complicated lies to smoke crack alone as often as I could afford it.

I didn't know what I wanted, but I knew it wasn't this. I'm a failure and so lost.

I called up my dad.

"Sure, come back to Minnesota. You can go to school here and live with me." Over the years, Dad had survived a couple of heart attacks, and I told my brothers that if I didn't make this move, I'd never get to know him. He was a "weekend dad" growing up, but I needed more now.

I flew up, and a Minnesota snowstorm greeted me the very next morning, just weeks after the thirty-inch Halloween Blizzard of 1991. I was buried in snow while the day before, I'd been paddling in the ocean, riding warm waves under the sun. I'd said goodbye to David and trusted him to hold on to my Spectrum surfboard for me. (Years later, I'd find out that he pawned it for drugs.) He was on his way to Fort Myers to live with Mom, while I'd headed north to make something of myself.

I walked into the admissions office at Minneapolis Technical College, ready to enroll. When the lady behind the desk asked, "Did you finish high school?" I lied. And when she requested a transcript, I innocently said, "Well, I went to Foley High in Alabama, so that's a problem." There had been a fire at my old school, and I bluffed, "All they'll be able to tell you is that I attended, but all their paper records got burned." The college would accept me, but I had to take a few placement exams first. I must have remembered enough from my high school days because I was officially accepted into their culinary program, complete with my very own chef's coat. Every quarter, there was a different focus—from baking to running a small restaurant to managing inventory, and even the fine art of five-star dining. I excelled through them all with As and Bs.

I paid my way through culinary school with loans, grants, and my work as a breakfast cook at the Hyatt, the perfect gig for someone with extreme energy. We sometimes served three hundred guests on Saturday mornings, and I'd have five or six omelet pans going at once. I opened drawers with my right foot, closed them with my knees, one hand cracked eggs while the other artistically plated an entrée. I'd found my place, where I belonged.

A few days a year, I channeled that energy into helping at high-profile entertainment shows at the International Market Square with my brother, Tim. I was the mic guy. I saw Donald and Ivanka Trump, MC Hammer, and Janet Jackson. They'd wait in a private area with security, and I'd radio Tim, "Two minutes till showtime." The performers would follow me to the curtain, and I'd call out, "Five, four, three, two, one, you're on!" They would stride onto the stage, and when they shouted, "Hey, everybody!" the crowd would go wild. It was an adrenaline rush.

On graduation day, Mom flew up to Minneapolis to watch me cross the stage and proudly accept my culinary arts diploma. We rented the penthouse at the top of Dad's apartment building and threw a party. The night ended early with my first DUI at the age of twenty-two. My buddies and I were headed to a strip club when I turned onto a one-way, the wrong way.

I was mad I'd gotten caught. They sat me down in a drunk tank in Hennepin County Jail, a large horseshoe-shaped room with no beds. The other drunks were sleeping it off on the floor, and I watched in disgust as an older gentleman in the cell next door was taking his feces in hand and smearing it across the window between us. I was required to attend a Mothers Against Drunk

Driving panel where families shared stories of lost loved ones because a driver had been drunk or high. That same night, I went through our cupboards and poured out every last drop of alcohol. I just wish the effect had lasted.

A few months later, after another night of partying, I snuck in around 3 a.m. I didn't want to wake Dad. My day started early as the breakfast cook at the Hyatt, and I was late getting up. I rushed to get out the door for work. When I came home that afternoon, the light was on over the table. Dad never left the light on; it got too hot. I lingered in the hallway, listening for movement before walking into the living room. I thought maybe the toilet had backed up when I smelled sewage. Then, from the corner of my eye, I saw him. He was sitting upright on the couch, not moving. I cried out, "Dad! Dad!" His head was tilted back, eyes wide open, his tongue sticking out, and his arms just hanging there, limp. I punched a wall and collapsed onto the floor in disbelief. I rocked back and forth, struggling to catch my breath, till I finally accepted I had to make the calls.

An ambulance showed up and then the coroner. They squeezed him into a long, black plastic bag, but when they lifted him from the couch, his head rolled back and smacked the ground with a sickening thud. That sound still haunts me. When a person dies, fluids drip from their body. The smell was my dad slowly rotting away.

What bothers me still is he could have been dead the night before. But I'd been wasted. I passed out, missed my alarm, and ran out of there. I just don't know. Dad took little nitroglycerin pills whenever his chest would hurt. Usually, he kept the bottle in his pocket, but that day, it was sitting on the table, tipped over. He'd already survived two heart attacks, and I think as he was trying to get a pill, he had another one. And that's what killed him.

Dad and I shared one TV, and he often set it to the channel displaying the apartment camera feeds. There were working girls around. When Dad was bored, he'd get caught up in the gossip of who was coming in and out, how this girl must have two boyfriends, and did you see that guy sneaking out behind her... It was like his own personal reality TV show. The day I found him, our lobby door was plastered on the TV screen. That meant he'd stayed up, waiting for me, watching for me. And I hadn't been there.

I moved into an apartment near Dad's old place and stuck to the same routine: Every night after work, we'd hit up bars along Lyndale Avenue, bouncing between Mortimer's and Rudoloph's. There'd be an after-party at someone's house, but I'd always make my way home. I had dreams of working at the prestigious Four Seasons in New York or the 510 in Minneapolis. Two of the greatest five-star restaurants at the time in any magazine. They served elaborate six-course meals, French haute cuisine at its finest, with crisp, freshly laundered linens gently placed on your lap. And before the main meal, they'd serve sorbet to cleanse your palette. It wasn't just dinner; it was a fucking experience.

I applied at the 510, where the wealthiest people in the state dined every weekend. It turned out the current chef was on his way out, and Joe Kaplan, who happened to be a young Jewish boy, a recent graduate of the Culinary Institute of America, was in. He was looking for a sous-chef and he hired me—a recent graduate of the small technical college down the block. I worked all the hours I could and focused on pork tenderloins instead of my dad lying in a body bag. Joe and I would roll the meat in pistachios and tarragon and stuff them with figs, chives, bacon, and walnuts. We'd whip up a cabernet glaze with a reduction of wine, fresh herbs, shallots, and garlic. Joe even taught me how to create stunning classical pâtés and terrines and arrange them on mirrors. On special holidays, we were booked out a year in advance. My brother, Tim, and his girlfriend came by the restaurant for dinner one night too. He smiled at me—the sous-chef—and I could see how proud he was.

The *Star Tribune* referred to us as the two Jews who had transformed the 510. We made it into the national *Gourmet* magazine, our faces featured in a spread. We were even on local TV as guest chefs—"Let's give a big welcome to Joe and Rory from the 510!" It boosted my ego to hear the crowd chanting my name as I flambéed a rack of lamb with a splash of cognac.

One night after work, knowing I'd have to wake up in a few hours to get the stocks and sauces going, I couldn't resist following the crowd to an after-party. I snorted a line of coke and breathed in deep as it lessened the grief, but it wasn't enough to keep me from asking, "Hey, you guys want to see something? Hand me a spoon. Do you have baking soda?" I worked my magic with the lighter, and they watched as I turned coke into a tiny rock, and when I took a hit of that crack, I didn't know how badly I'd needed it. I didn't want to remember the foul smell or the zipper closing over Dad. Mostly, I wanted the echo of that damn thud to stop. As I blew out the smoke, the world paused, the pain left, and I had everything I could ever dream of.

It takes just one night like mine to change your whole life. Or maybe just five minutes of kneeling in front of a cardboard box with a spoon and a lighter in a rented room. Crack didn't do anything for the guys around me or for Mom or David. Wasn't for them, but it was for *me*. I'd been able to smoke on and off, taking breaks, but with this particular hit, I was reeling from the death of my dad. I'd found a cure. That's what's scary about drugs. You never know what your body will love in that moment…and then you'll do anything to keep that high going. It was like finding the perfect woman made just for me, who gave me exactly what I wanted, how I wanted it, every single time. But I always came down, and when it was over, I was left grieving a broken relationship.

After that night, the chase was on.

With the cash from each paycheck from the 510 in hand, I drove straight to Lake and Third Streets in downtown Minneapolis. The first night I pulled up to the corner, I handed over a twenty to a dealer and watched as he walked into the house behind him to get my dope, only to see him run out the back door. I never saw him or my twenty again. I could have invited him inside my car for the exchange, but he might have pulled something on me and taken my money anyway. I quickly learned it was safest to go through the working girls for crack. They'd use the chance to lure me into a date, but at least they wouldn't run off with my money when I said no.

After a few weeks, I went straight to the source—the local dope houses. Two dealers from Detroit, Pony and G, would bus in young kids from their hometown dressed in Nike jumpsuits and fresh Pumas. These kids would be assigned a specific dope house where they were given a plate and a pistol-grip shotgun. They became the servers. Pony and G would bring them "onions," large amounts of crack, and the kids would sit on the couch for forty-eight to seventy-two hours at a time, cutting and serving up the dope.

Inside each house, it was the doorman's job to yell out, "Custo!" when he'd see a customer rolling up. He'd tell them to come in quickly, that there were cops circling, and get them all paranoid. The doorman would ask how much they needed and get the right amount from the server to hand over. He'd do so, but not before transferring some of the dope into his own pocket.

Even if the customer suspected they were getting ripped off, they'd be too scared to hang around.

Sometimes, I'd act as the lookout at one of these houses. I'd sit in the upstairs bedroom, peeking out from behind a curtain cracked half an inch, and watch the road. I'd take a hit, blow out the smoke, get *stuck*, and just stare out the window. Twenty-four hours at a time. If I suspected anything, I'd holler, "Raid!" The server would dump the plate of dope over a Folgers coffee can filled with Drano. By the time the cops demanded, "Where's the dope?!" it had already sizzled and dissolved away. Pony and G would make their rounds, moving from crack house to crack house, to fill the plates back up and collect the cash. Meanwhile, the guy who actually owned the house would be lying in a corner, hooked and high in exchange.

When I was offered a higher-paying job as a sous-chef at the Interlachen Country Club in Edina, Minnesota, I took a hard look at myself in the bathroom mirror and knew I had to sober up. I was now serving wealthy superstars like the owner of the Minnesota Twins. But my need was just too strong.

One afternoon, I got a bigger rock, a couple hundred bucks worth. I hopped into my Honda and drove straight to Lake Minnetonka. It was winter, and I pulled right up onto the ice. If the cops showed up, my plan was to toss the drugs out the window and watch it disappear into the snow around me. I took a hit and whipped my car around to see if they were coming. I looked left, then right, watching, waiting. With a second hit, I spun the car another forty-five degrees, my eyes darting back and forth. Over and over again. A state of insanity and paranoia. I was White Boy Fred, stuck like Chuck.

I went downhill fast. I used my paycheck for three things: rent, food, and crack. When money got tight, I moved in with a coworker from the country club. On days off, I'd get high, and it wasn't long before I was calling in sick. I had burn marks along my fingers from holding a hot pipe one too many times. My lips were covered in blisters, crusted over with dried blood. The tell-tale signs of a crackhead. I'd spend my days popping out the inner lining of my pants pocket, double- and triple-checking for the tiniest white rock. Or I'd dig around ashtrays or the dirt, thinking I might have dropped the smallest, most precious piece. Sometimes, I'd surf the carpet for hours, running my fingers through the grooves and ridges of every fiber. And then I'd do it again because I was still holding out hope.

When my roommate caught me in his basement taking hits of crack through a toilet paper roll and dryer sheets, he kicked me out. "I know what you're doing, and I don't want that shit in my house."

I pictured my roommate sharing my darkest secret with the other chefs and was too ashamed to show my face at work again. In less than a year since Dad had died, I lost my place, I lost my job, I maxed out my credit cards, and moved into my car. Just me and my crack pipe. My body couldn't function without the drug anymore. I'd feel too much, and the craving would overwhelm me.

When I was a boy, I had dreams; living the life of a homeless crackhead wasn't it. Years ago, during family dinners, Aunt Sylvia would ask me to lead the Passover meal. I'd politely say, "Of course, Aunt Sylvia. But you know, this isn't set up exactly right. The seder plate should be on the other side of..." I'd continue while rearranging. My brothers would mock me from behind, but she'd smile down at me and give my head a little pat. "Oh, thank you, Rory. You're such a good Jewish boy."

Now, I parked my car down the street from her house, banged on the door, and lied. "Hey, Aunt Syliva. It's good to see you too.

Listen, my car got towed, and I need sixty dollars to bail it out." I stood and watched as she grabbed her purse without a second thought. I felt sick, but it didn't stop me from trying a similar trick on her son, my cousin, Jimmy, but he didn't buy it. He walked me down to his basement to talk; probably didn't want me around his family. He knew. "Who did you say is after you? Why don't I have my friend who works down at the police station investigate for you?"

I never trusted myself to ask anyone, "Hey, can I stay at your place while I get my life together?" Even when I'd tried to stay sober, I'd be back at it as soon as I had a little money. It wasn't about being ready to quit. I didn't know what I wanted, *but I knew it wasn't this.* I'd made the decision to stop, but crack had such a hold on me. And as long as it did, man, the shit I would do and the choices I would make to get it, the stealing and all the lying... No. I decided I wasn't going near anyone, especially my family. Not my brothers. And definitely not my mom.

I'm a failure and lost. I'm a bad person too.

Rory, around age twenty

43

(From left to right) Raymond, Arnell, David, and Rory

Rory receives his culinary arts diploma

Rory with Joe Kaplan (right) at the 510

LIFE ON REPEAT

When I couldn't see another option, I was desperate enough to negotiate with my dealers: Pony and G could use my Honda if I could crash in the basement of one of their crack houses. During the day, with nowhere good to go, I'd walk the block where I started a habit of picking fights with bar-goers. I didn't just sit there with a glass in front of me and my head down. Oh no, I'd go to the biggest guy in the joint, give his chest a little tap, and slur out, "What's your problem?" He'd tower over me and breathe into the top of my head, "What are you, fucking stupid?" Bam! And I'd be knocked out.

When I landed in detox, the counselor transferred me to my first treatment center at Pine Shores in Pine City, Minnesota. Each time, centers and jails offered me a moment of clarity, a chance to reset and get the chemicals out of my system. On the streets, I was caught inside an obsessive tornado, compulsively going around and around over my next hit or drink. *Oh, how the ice cubes will clink against the glass when I pour a shot of rum. How I'll raise the rim to my dry lips where my tongue will tingle at the first touch of the cold liquid, warming my insides as it slides down.* To anyone else, it was just a fucking drink. But for me, I was caught up in a fantasy...a whirlwind romance, blinded by love.

Now, I was removed from the eye of the storm and dropped into a new environment. There was heat, and people were kind and let me borrow their clothes. The staff would try to teach me tools to manage my cravings and get me thinking about my reasons for using, but I'm not sure how much I really heard. Those first two weeks, I was just getting back to reality. Only after I got food in my stomach and gained some weight back did I feel good about myself again and could think about better decisions.

When they asked, "Do you want to get your high school diploma?" I paused. I usually spat out my high-school-burned-down story, but I swallowed my words. In treatment, they drilled us to be rigorously honest, with others and ourselves. So, at the age of twenty-four, I walked into a Pine City High School classroom, squeezed myself into a student desk, and focused all my study prep into the GED exam in front of me. And guess what? I passed.

As I got healthier both physically and mentally, I became Pine Shores' star student, dedicated to the program. At every center I've been to, I got compliments. My peers would tell me, "Out of all of us, if any one person makes it, it's going to be you." Maybe I did well because I found a place to rest for a moment, a place where I belonged.

On my last day there, Pony came to pick me up in my car. I turned to the Detroit dealer and firmly said, "You know what, Pony? It's my turn now. My turn to make money. I'm done getting high."

We drove straight to his dope house where he placed a mound of crack in front of me and said, "Okay, Fred, you're our new server." Alright, hook me up. I started bagging it up as customers came rolling through with cash burning holes in their pockets. With a chuckle, I thought, "I'm never going to use now. I'm cured. I'm okay."

I strolled down to the gas station for cigarettes, and on my way back through the alleyway, I sipped some pop, dumped the rest, and crushed the can in the middle. Like a magician with a sleight of hand, I took a key, popped a hole in the can, flicked my cigarette ash onto it, broke off a piece of crack, and took a hit. My happiest moment times a hundred.

Two hours ago, I was skipping from the treatment center and handing out high fives. It took just thirty seconds to erase those thirty days. The counselor had asked if I wanted to go to a halfway house to live sober with support. "Oh, no, no, no. I'm good," I'd said.

I got back to the dope house but didn't stop. I couldn't. I could hear Pony shouting behind me, "Fred, you did, didn't you?! Man!" He knew I'd broken—that I *was broken*—by just looking at me. I wandered toward the I-35W bridge and stared hard at the Mississippi River below. If I couldn't quit this, then screw it. I wasn't ever going to beat this thing. I gripped the railing, but in my heart I knew that while I didn't want to live this way, I didn't want to die, either.

I fumbled for my wallet and searched the pockets till I found the number to the halfway house they'd told me to hang onto that morning. I got to a pay phone, and with shaky hands, I made the call. There was an opening in Hastings, Minnesota, a place called the Cochran House. I sobbed into the phone, "I'll go, I'll go, I'll go. I need to get out of here. I'm not doing good. I have nowhere else to fucking go." They'd have a room ready for me on Monday.

At the Cochran House, minutes turned into hours, hours turned into days, days turned into weeks, and I stayed sober. One warm afternoon, Mom visited, and we spread a blanket in a park near a bridge where people were fishing. She talked about Vinny Barbarino, her handsome Italian boyfriend who owned a deli in Fort Myers, Florida. He treated her well and had taken her on a dream trip to Italy. She'd mailed me a postcard with a picture of their hotel, their room circled in ink. I shared about my stays at detox and treatment centers, but not the depth of it. I was too ashamed to tell anyone the truth about the things I'd seen and done for my drug. I wanted her to be happy.

When I felt strong enough, I walked into the Levee Cafe along the Mississippi River and applied for a job. As they scanned my résumé, they questioned, "You've worked at the Hyatt, the 510, and the Interlachen Country Club too? A trained sous-chef certified through the American Culinary Federation. And you want to work in our café?" They were worried they couldn't pay me enough. I openly admitted I was living at the halfway house and just needed to stay busy. One of the owners was a sports bookie with a gambling addiction, just released from prison. He understood.

I was thankful for the work, even if it meant starting from the bottom. I quickly impressed them with my sauces, including a cherries jubilee poured over vanilla ice cream. It wasn't long before I asked for a tableside flambé cart. In the evenings, I'd stroll the dining room, cooking up bananas Foster and lighting shit on fire to rounds of applause. The owner whispered, "Dude, it's never been like this." On Friday and Saturday nights, we now had a line of people waiting to get in. If they thought this was something, they should have seen me with a watermelon. I could whip and swish my knife around and present a kitten playing with a ball of yarn or a dove with an olive branch.

When I was promoted to head chef at Levee's, I started dating

Diane, one of the waitresses there. With the money I'd saved, I left the halfway house and got my own place. I hadn't touched crack since that night on the bridge, but I'd started drinking again. One night after work, I had a Bacardi Coke to relax. I knew I had one too many because a switch flipped inside me as it always did on the third round. I was done with the rum and colas, and what I craved was a hit of crack. I didn't want meth. I didn't want heroin. I didn't want to gamble. I didn't want a girl. Right then, more than anything in the world, I wanted crack. I knew exactly the high it would give me—so perfect because it never let me down.

I'd been hiding my Honda from the repo man in a storage unit under Diane's name. It was Saturday night, and I had the next two days off. The timing was perfect. I pulled out the car and drove forty-five minutes to Dale Street in Saint Paul to find the working girls. It was so easy to slip back into smooth-talking White Boy Fred. "Hey, what up baby, heyyy. I just wanna get some rock. I'll take care of you real good. I'll pay you, I'll share with you, whatever. We can hang out."

"Yeah, yeah, little white boy. I'll give you some crack. How much you have?"

I made a show of pulling out a twenty, making sure she could see the couple of fifties behind it. I flashed them long enough to do the job. See, with just a ten or twenty, she'd take my money and I'd never see her again. But with the promise of more, I could get her to actually come back with a rock. "C'mon, baby, I got a bunch more here. I wanna party with you all night." I was a salesman and had it down to a science. I knew exactly where to go, what to do, and what to say to get me my fucking rock. And once I had it in my hands, I slipped away with her voice trailing behind me.

"Hey, baby, what? You don't like me?"

I yelled back, "It ain't like that, baby! It's all good." I picked up my pace, itching for a hit.

I started driving to Dale Street every weekend. On the way back one night, I saw flashing lights behind me. I slipped the rock under my tongue and moved it around my mouth as I waited in jail. I was charged with my second DUI, sentenced to four months, and lost my getaway car. When I was released on probation, I was required to attend a treatment program four nights a week in a town thirty minutes away, while maintaining my job in Hastings. The courts knew my story, that I couldn't drive and didn't have any family around. Still, I hitchhiked there a couple of nights, but it was winter and I couldn't keep that going. They wrote up a violation of the conditions of my release, and I had to do another thirty days. It felt impossible to succeed.

When I got out, I couldn't face the shame of leaving the owners at Levee's hanging again, so I just never went back. By then, Diane, my girlfriend, was long gone too. In dope houses, I watched the line of people waiting to buy meth grow, and I needed work; I decided to be a meth dealer. I'd tried meth once and was amped for days. Compulsively vacuuming in the middle of the night. I hated being on high alert; my euphoria was the quiet and stillness of crack. But all the young girls loved meth and called it "the Jenny Crank" diet because they'd stay thin and still have energy to burn.

With my little pot of savings, I rented a place in Hastings and started up my own dope house. Five months ago, I was flambéing bananas Foster from a tableside chef's cart; now I served up meth scooped from little sandwich baggies.

Every week, Alma, a cute seventeen-year-old girl, would come to buy weed. She towered over me at six foot one and would flip back her long black hair when she spoke. Her friends would walk in first, giggling through the door, saying, "She likes you, you know." I knew because once, when I peeked in Alma's purse, I saw all of last week's weed still there, and she was already back for more. But she was young, and I knew myself. I wasn't a good person. I'd end up hurting her. When Alma walked in on her eighteenth birthday and danced around with her friends, I told myself, "Don't just screw her. She's cool. She's fun. Get to know her." We got wasted on tequila, and I woke up the next morning with Alma lying next to me. We hung out every day after that, and I listened as she shared her dreams of signing a modeling contract. If that didn't work out, she had plans to enter basic training with the Air Force to become an air traffic controller.

One evening, I was bagging up the latest delivery of dope when I saw Alma pulling up to the house. She got out and stood next to her baby blue car, holding on to its roof to keep steady. When she turned her face toward me, I saw tears rolling down her cheeks. She didn't have to say a word. I felt what she came there to tell me.

"What should I do?" she asked.

I told her, "Alma, in the state of Minnesota, it's not up to me. All I can say is, if you decide to have this baby, I'll do everything I can as the father to be there for our child."

I was only twenty-six but I had a plan. I moved a buddy and his girl into my dope house, and they sold ten- to twenty-dollar bags for me. With the cash rolling in, I rented a penthouse downtown above an attorney's office with gorgeous walkways. This was the place Alma and the baby would come home to when Sabina was born on June 16, 1997. At the hospital, when I walked over for a closer look, she'd taken a little swing at me. A natural-born fighter. I kept Sabina near me, day and night, while Alma worked at Treasure Island Casino as a security guard. I didn't want Sabina in day care, not when she couldn't come home and tell me what really happened that day.

Three years prior, I'd been living homeless on the streets of Minneapolis, and now I had a dope house and a penthouse. I could facilitate, delegate, and manage people. When Sabina slept, the penthouse became a revolving door for my bigger clients. Girls were coming and going. With cash flowing in, I smoked crack every chance I got behind Alma's back. I made it a point never to smoke around my family. While her parents watched Sabina, I'd lie, sneak, and disappear for a day or two, hiding out at a motel. Alma still believes I cheated on her, and it didn't look good, but I never did. It was just me and my crack pipe. The distance between Alma and me grew. We had fun together and loved and respected each other, but we were never soulmates. We had entered an arrangement just like my parents had.

When Sabina was five months old, doctors found cancer in my mom's lungs. It knocked my legs out from under me. They'd attempted to remove it, but it was too late. The cancer had spread. Alma and I packed a suitcase and flew down to Fort Myers with Sabina so she could meet her. Mom adjusted her tubes and made space to hold my little girl on her bed. That was the last time we saw her.

They say you never get more than you can handle. Explain that one to me. Then Grandpa died a year later. The three people who meant everything to me were gone. Taken.

We let the penthouse go, and Alma and I moved into a smaller apartment. As one last attempt to save our relationship, I checked myself into treatment at a hospital in the next town. But hours after I left, I was back on crack again. Alma and I fought one night—pushing and grabbing and pulling. The cops pounded on the door and demanded I leave. That was the start of Alma and I going our separate ways.

I went back to living out of my dope house again. Ironically, it was right across from the police station. I made sure the door opened outward so no one could kick their way in. But that didn't keep me from almost dying one night.

I heard a knock at the door, and when I looked through the peephole, I saw Chris from the pizza place across the street give a small wave. As soon as I opened it, he took a long step back and two men in camouflage hunting gear rushed toward me with a lead pipe. They split my head open and knocked me to the ground, pounding my ribs over and over with their steel-toed boots. One climbed onto my back and kept punching my neck and head. Adrenaline kicked in, and I stood with his weight still on me. But a hard kick to my gut from the other guy knocked me right back down.

When I finally came to, they were gone. The door was wide open, and I watched a cop car slowly drive by. The officer stopped when he saw me and rolled down his window. I told him I'd gotten into it with a friend, assured him I was fine, and he left.

I called my buddy, Robert, and frantically told him I'd been attacked. He doctored me over the phone. "Don't worry about your ribs, man. Stop the bleeding on your head. You can't have a head wound. Dude, you're gonna have to go to the hospital." He'd been drinking, so he sent his roommate to drive me to the ER. I had a fractured arm and broken ribs. Staples crisscrossed my head. When I turned over in my hospital bed, I saw the same cop who had questioned me earlier smirking in the doorframe. How peculiar. I grunted as the pieces clicked into place. I wanted to cry out, "You checking up on me, making sure your fucking friends or family didn't kill me when they jumped me? What, their cuts get too tight with me in town? Don't fucking look at me, you fuck. May whatever you all have coming come your fucking way."

For the next ten days, I sat in my dope house with a loaded shotgun in my lap, twacked out on meth. I couldn't afford to get *stuck* on crack; I'd be a sitting duck. I told Chris to shove his pizza up his ass and pass on a message for me: "I have some chips and dip on the table. Your buddies can come on by and get a little snack. I'll be waiting for them." When clients walked in, they'd take in my crazed eyes shifting in every direction as I peered closely at faces, my fist around my shotgun. They'd U-turn right out and buy their dope somewhere else. I was losing my mind, and it was time to go.

Robert invited me to stay with him. He had his own past—he'd robbed thirteen banks before the cops caught him at the racetrack and arrested him. He served his time in Folsom and San Quentin, and nowadays drank vodka at 9 a.m. I slumped on his couch, took his cue, and drank Bacardi from sunup to sundown for a month straight.

One night, I was driving back from Treasure Island on a back road in my Lincoln Town Car. I just wanted to get to bed after losing a pile of cash. When I saw the speed trap, I slowed right down but the cop caught up to me. I'd been drinking all night with a tumbler full of Bacardi Coke right next to me. I knew my breath reeked. With two prior DUIs, it was a done deal. I never showed up to court to face the charge.

Crack. Treatment at Pine Shores. Crack. Treatment at the Cochran House. Crack. Treatment in Red Wing. Crack. When would I learn? I knew it couldn't be scared out of me. If it could, it would have happened years ago in Minneapolis on the roughest night of my life, long before I ever got jumped.

I remember standing inside a Crips' dope house when a bunch of Bloods women walked in. Two of the toughest gang rivals in the city under one roof. The women waved twenty-dollar bills around to show they were going to buy some rock, but they were really there to scope the place out. It was a typical crack house with a doorman, a lookout, and a server with a .38-caliber revolver in his lap. The way these girls were talking, "Heeeey, guys! Let's hang tonight!" we knew something was going down.

Minutes later, bullets screamed past us. The lookout shut the lights off, and I crouched low against a wall. *Pop, pop, pop, pop, pop!* I covered my ears and protected my head as glass shattered around me. When it finally got quiet, I slowly looked around. It wasn't dark anymore. I was sitting in moonlight shining through a bullet hole, just inches above where my head had been.

And here I was, still lost as ever. Twenty-nine years old and living on a friend's couch. I needed a fresh start. I got my answer when Robert and I strolled past a "be all you can be" poster. I thought, why not? I met with an army recruit, took their test, and walked like a duck in my boxers. When they checked my hearing, I placed in the top three highest scores ever.

They didn't know about the years I'd spent in basements and motel bathrooms smoking crack—hunkered down, quiet, paranoid of the cops, my ear to the door. Listening. The drugs would be in my fist, my index finger on the flush of the toilet, always ready. Ten hours of waiting for a moving shadow. When the high wore off, I'd have to pry each finger open one at a time, and a half-melted piece of crack would fall from my palm. I'd be so fucking paranoid to ever take a second hit. Just waiting, watching, listening.

I thought I'd make my dad proud—he'd served in his day—and maybe find my place in the world. I'd always done well with structure, at school and in treatment. But when they red-flagged my scoliosis, they were sorry to inform me that I was disqualified from ever enlisting. I was desperate for direction; I had carried my last shred of hope into that office. Now that was gone too.

By then, I'd blown through my savings. When I overheard my buddy, Tony, joke that his friend's mom was a waitress who kept her tip change in cookie tins, I immediately began crafting a plan. The very next night, I picked the lock and broke into her house when she was working. The tins were exactly where Tony said they'd be, and I dumped them into a backpack. I remember the weight as I spun the bag onto my shoulders. I laid low at Tony's for a few days and alternated between drinking and smoking crack.

One morning, I caught Tony and his wife staring at me wide-eyed, in shock. When I sprang from the couch, we saw streaks of red across the cushion. I had blood coming out of my insides, from my ass and my penis. Extreme alcoholism at work. Out of mercy, Tony's wife dropped me in front of Dakota County Jail, knowing there was a warrant out for my arrest. She just wanted me to get the medical help I desperately needed. Tremors passed through my body as it detoxed off rum and everything else.

I signed up to work off my jail sentence in a Sentencing to Service program. The other inmates and I cut down trees along the road near Dunwoody College, and on weekends, we chewed tobacco, munched on sugary snacks, and ran gambling boards during football games. We took part in everything that was smuggled in during the week. When my time was up in 2000, I wanted to get the fuck out of Hastings where I was nearly beaten to death. I volunteered to go to the Pathway House in Rochester,

Minnesota. After one last night of freedom at the casino, I arrived to treatment high and hungover.

From my second-story room at Pathways, I had a clear view of the Mayo Clinic and downtown Rochester. The moment I saw the Kahler Grand Hotel, I remembered how Mom and I had stayed there once when I was a kid. She'd bought me a little magic kit with a vase of flowers I could turn upside down, and miraculously, the water wouldn't drip out. At thirty, I was back in the same town, alone, where there was nothing magical about the Breathalyzer and urine test they gave me. To this day, I don't know why Pathways ever allowed me a bed with the amount I'd drank the night before.

I overheard guys complaining, "Man, this is bullshit. The food sucks here, and you gotta smoke outside?" I'd just gotten out of jail and wanted to say, "You guys have a salad bar here. And you can have seconds? What are you whining about?!" In jail, they'd nicknamed me Tapeworm because I was always hungry. At mealtime, I would sit by the garbage cans and catch the other inmates before they scraped off their leftovers. A lot of them wouldn't eat their veggies, so I'd end up with large piles on my tray. With a little salt and pepper, I'd devour them. My roommate probably hated me for it—full of fiber and hogging the shitter.

I successfully finished treatment, as I usually did. I even got a sponsor this time, but I only had to follow the pattern to know what was next: Crack. Pine Shores. Crack. Cochran House. Crack. Red Wing. Crack. Pathway House. I met a guy who removed ice dams from roofs for Rob's Construction. He told me I could make up to $150 a day and brought me in. It was just a matter of time before I found the crack dealers behind the downtown bars and burned through the dough. Then I bounced from one buddy's house to the next, many with the same demons. Together, we would find temp jobs through Labor Ready, make forty-five bucks a piece, buy a rock and a bottle of Bacardi, and cook up two packs of ramen to make it through the day. Over and over and over. *I didn't know what I wanted, but it sure as hell wasn't this.*

The same story. *I'm a failure, lost, and a bad person. I'm defective.*

It was just months later, on March 20, 2001, that I wandered into that SuperAmerica gas station.

FORK IN THE ROAD

Back in the darkened motel room, I saw my picture flash across the TV. I was alone again, the last nail already in my coffin: *Olmsted County's Most Wanted Man, Rory Londer.* I slumped down on the bed, sagging at the center, and pulled out my wallet. There was a picture of my daughter. She was three years old now. I hadn't seen her much since I'd moved to Rochester. Alma had brought her around a few times at Pathways, but she could see it in my eyes when I started getting high again. She knew better and just stayed away.

I held Sabina's picture in my hand and did the math. I could disappear in some small corner of a town in Florida for seven years, avoid extradition, and then come back. Or, I could do two years for aggravated robbery and be back in my daughter's life while she was still little. Finally, as a dirtbag father, it mattered to me. One of the only good things in my life was getting to see my girl. She'd hang onto me with her arms wrapped tightly around my neck. When she hugged me, it was from the heart, and that warmth would run straight through me.

For my third DUI, when I sat in jail, Sabina would visit me. The moment she caught a glimpse of me, she'd turn her whole body toward me and smile so wide it reached her eyes. For me, she was sunlight breaking through dark clouds. Looking at me through a sheet of glass between us, she'd pick up the telephone. *Hi, Daddy.* Such sweet innocence. I wrote to her every day. I'd sketch out a flower in a certain color on the bottom corner of the envelope and copy it exactly like that onto the paper inside. I created my own stationery, using a different colored pencil each time to make it special for her.

I reached for the phone now and dialed my sponsor's number. "So what do you think I should do, Glen?"

"You should listen to yourself. You've already said what you're going to do."

Would she be five years old or ten before I saw her again? I'd been thinking about robbing Eastwood Bank off Highway 14 for a while. Maybe I'd do that and then run to Florida, if the cops didn't catch me first. With my thumb, I caressed Sabina's face, grasping hard at the photograph, the only thing left that gave me an ounce of worth.

When the crack wore off and the booze kicked in, I slowly dialed 911.

"I'm sitting here at Econo Lodge. I'm the guy who robbed the SA." They told me to come down and turn myself in. "I'm fucking high as shit. I'm not going anywhere. You come and get me."

"What's your room number?"

I looked down at my bottle of rum and hung up without answering. If I was going to prison, I was having myself one more drink. I cleaned up, packed my backpack, and filled my glass. Then I moved to the edge of the bed and waited.

BOOM! The door kicked in. "Down! Down! Get down now!" A stun grenade rolled across the floor and a blinding, ear-shattering flash of white followed. A trail of smoke clouded the room. There I was, just sitting on my bed, clutching my backpack like a schoolchild waiting to be led by hand for my consequence. They brought me down with a knee to my neck. They were doing their job, acting off the information they had—a guy high on crack just robbed a gas station at gunpoint and was now hiding out in a motel room. "Where's the gun?" they shouted. "Where is it?! Tell us where it is!"

I squeaked out, "I don't have one! I swear! I used my fingers and pretended like I did!" They handcuffed me and dragged me to a cop car and we sped off to the station. As we walked toward the questioning room, I saw my face on TV with the words, "SA Bandit Strikes Again," in all caps below. I pieced together that some other guy was robbing SuperAmericas all around the county. When a cop pushed me down into a chair and spat out, "Where were you on the night of…" I rushed to my defense. "No, no! I only did this once! I swear, I only robbed the one SA!" It didn't take them long to compare the video footage; the other guy was obviously much taller.

They led me to my jail cell and assigned me a public defender. She was a young woman who just laughed. "So let me get this straight. You rob a gas station with your finger and then tell on yourself. What were you thinking?" My story was simple. I was high on crack and needed the money. We went back and forth to court a few times, and the prosecutor tried to argue it was a real gun, but it didn't stick. They reduced the charge to a simple robbery, a felony offense.

When I retrace my steps from that night at the SA, I think I wanted to get caught. I didn't even try to disguise my face. I wasn't a master thief, but I've threatened, intimidated, and robbed people before, pawning things I'd grab from open garages, and I always covered my tracks. I knew how to find a generic, size twelve shoe at the Salvation Army and duct tape the bottom so they wouldn't leave any prints. They would assume I was bigger than I was, and I'd have gloves, a hat, a mask, anything to throw them off. But at the SA, I had a full fucking conversation with the kid. After jail cells, detox centers, treatment centers, and halfway houses—blowing from one to the next, *wanting something different, but not knowing how*—I still couldn't stop. It was crack cocaine versus Rory, and crack always won. I just didn't care anymore.

Locked inside my jail cell, I kept reliving the night I was arrested and the moment the cops hauled me out of the motel in handcuffs. I replayed that scene over and over, a twisted form of punishment. I remembered squinting from the flashing lights of a fire truck and an ambulance. As they led me toward the cop car, from the corner of my eye, I saw an older man reach an arm out to shield his wife, protecting her from me. That cut so deep. What had I become?

I'm unlovable.

***

That night of the SA Bandit—March 20, 2001—marked the beginning of my first long stretch of sobriety. Since then, I've sponsored hundreds of men. I tell them, at first, we choose to use because of the effects produced by the drug. Later, we use because of the effects produced when we don't fucking have it. When it turns on you and becomes more powerful. Something you can't live without.

When I met Steve, one of my first sponsees, he had relapsed after a recent divorce. He straightened his baseball cap before starting in on everything wrong in his life. I handed him a slip of paper. "Here's my phone number. If you start calling it, I'll answer." We talked every day, sometimes more, because he didn't know how to get through a single day without using.

I would call him out to a worksite every Saturday morning, and as I hammered away on a remodel, he'd read aloud from *Alcoholics Anonymous*. One morning, he confided he was facing an old DUI charge and had to serve home detention. When he complained, "I gotta pay a hundred a week…it's bullshit," I was harsh because I had to be.

"No, it's bullshit that you got into your fucking car drunk and turned the key. You could have killed someone. Shut your mouth."

When he was on an ankle monitor, Steve called again. "It's day three, man, and I can't leave my fucking house. Can you at least bring me some Cokes or something?"

"Yeah, no problem," I promised. "I'll be off work in a couple hours and can swing by. No big deal." I pulled up on the street in front of his house and called out, "Steve! Hey!" I set the twelve-pack on the edge of his driveway and sped off, laughing as I caught a glimpse of him flipping me off in the rearview mirror. We both knew if he took one step closer, the alarm would go off.

I never lied to any of the guys I sponsored and said, "Everything's going to be okay." No, it's not. If you keep using, I'd say, it'll tear your family apart and wreck it, if it hasn't already. Your kids will be sitting alone on their birthday at nine o'clock at night, crying and wondering where the fuck you are. Your wife will leave and your kids will stop talking to you, and years later, you'll be sitting in a jail cell wondering if you're going to whack yourself or not because of all the pain you don't know how to carry any more. And you want me to tell you that everything's going to be okay? No, your addiction will grip you till it becomes a tornado through your life, through your family's life, and it will destroy everything in its path. In families, there are disagreements, but bringing alcohol or drugs into the mix adds fuel to the fire. You want to turn a guy or gal into an asshole? Just add alcohol. Their voice changes. The jabs begin. The other person's left thinking, "Who are you right now? You never talk like this to us. I'm not going to keep on keeping on."

You can be the nicest, sweetest, most established member in the community...but if there's something inside you that clicks into place when you down that drink or drug, like it does for me, you have two choices: You can ride it out till the very end—where maybe you have a little too much one night, or maybe you take a little bigger hit, and *bam*! You're gone. *Or, you can try something different.* I tell the men I sponsor, when you're ready to decide, let me know.

The story of my downward spiral isn't really much of a puzzle; it's an all-too-common one among men and women active in their addiction. And when people learn I've been sober since 2005— that I bought the laundromat I used to rest in on frigid nights and turned it into a million-dollar business—they follow up with an intrigued, "How did you do it?" I answer them, and you'll read about that later. But the heart of this book answers a different question people don't think to ask: How did I recover my self-worth, a belief in myself, after decades of living with the weight of shame? For decades, enduring thoughts that crushed me—*I'm a failure, I'm lost, I'm a bad person, I'm defective, I'm unlovable.* So how? How did I recover my value as a human being? How did I decide to keep trying after all of that?

What follows is *my something different.*

The photo Rory carried in his wallet of Sabina, age three

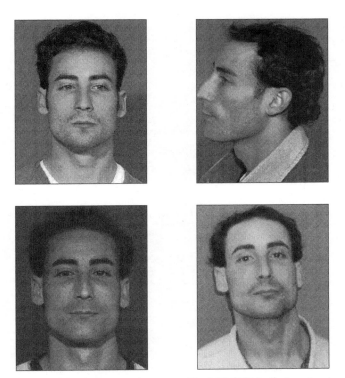

A few of Rory's mugshots leading up to his arrest on March 20, 2001 for the SuperAmerica robbery

THE PERSON WHO NEEDS IT MOST, WE HAVE TO LOVE THE HARDEST

After a routine meeting with my lawyer for the SA Bandit charge, I joined the other inmates in the common area. We were sitting around a TV screen when my chair was kicked hard from behind. I turned and immediately knew I couldn't take this guy. But it didn't stop me from getting to my feet and calling him out. "So, let me get this straight. The biggest motherfucker in this whole place is picking on me, the smallest motherfucker? On the littlest, skinniest, ninety-pound crackhead. That makes you the biggest bitch in here, man." He threw the first punch and we went at it till the guards maced us and put us in lockdown, our eyes swollen. Three days later, we came out of our cells, were told to get along, and we did. And no one bothered me again.

I was in jail long enough to get a job mopping the hallways. The worst was the booking area, where people were brought in after their arrests and would often piss on the floor, drunk. I was there cleaning, and when the other inmates were done for the night, on birthdays, the guards would pass pizza around and call me over. Once, over a piece of leftover cake, Sergeant Alfredo had a heart-to-heart when we finished comparing ways of making ceviche, with lemon versus champagne versus wine. Since he'd learned I was once a chef, we talked often. Now, he asked, "Rory, what are you doing? Looks like you're a smart kid, but this shit's really got a hold on you. You're a good guy, man. Come on." What he was really asking was, "Can't you try harder?" He treated me like a parent when mine were both dead.

The next time I went before a judge, I joked with the guys, "I should just walk in backward because I'm going to get fucked in the ass anyway." (I'd actually tried this back in Hastings. The judge threw his hands in the air, "You think you're the first asshole to do this? Thirty more days! Send him back.")

Judge Joseph Weiners, nicknamed old Let 'Em Go Joe, shuffled through my records and said, "Let me get this straight. You're a repeat DUI offender, but you robbed a gas station. You got high on crack, used your finger not a gun, and turned yourself in. I can't remember the last time a man sat in my courtroom and took responsibility for his actions to this level. Your problem's with drugs, and I don't think you need to be here one more day. Now, you'll be on probation for the next ten years, but you're going home. Do you have somewhere to go?"

I looked at him in shock and stuttered, "I-uh-can-um-I can find somewhere to go." After months in jail, I skipped back to my unit and yelled out, "I'm going home!" As I walked out, the other inmates banged against their metal cells and chanted, "Free the Jew! Free the Jew! Free the Jew!"

I stepped outside the Olmsted County Courthouse, picked up a half-smoked cigarette butt near the garbage can, and sat down on the top step. Before jail, I'd been couch-hopping. With no place to call home, my feet led me toward the Pioneer AA Club, where I'd gone a few times during treatment. I walked into the smoke-filled room that was lined with hand-me-down office chairs from the Mayo Clinic. Cigarette burns spotted the cloth seats. An older couple heard my story of how I was just out of jail and offered me a place to stay for a few nights. His wife made a cake to celebrate my release. I politely started with a small slice, and when she said not to be shy, I devoured half of it.

Feeling rested, I went down to the Dorothy Day House. Every day, companies would call temporary homeless shelters looking for workers. When I walked in, a voice behind the counter shouted, "Hey! Anyone wanna work at Rob's Construction?" I grabbed the phone from her. On the other end, Kenny, the owner, asked with surprise, "Who is this? Rory?! Yeah, I remember you! The ice dams. Where have you been, man?" I told him the truth: Remember the SA bandit on TV? Well…

Kenny picked me up the next morning for a job, and I left my culinary days behind for good. In the restaurant world, everyone goes out for a drink after work, and when you're tired, a little cocaine can go a long way. It was just too easy to be swept up with the crowd.

Every day, I got up, biked to work, and made time for an AA meeting. When days became a year sober, my sponsor gave me a push. "It's time, Rory, to help someone else. You know how you've been saying you want a relationship? Well, this is Charlie, your new girlfriend now."

Charlie was the first person I sponsored. He was six foot four with large, splotchy birthmarks down his arms. Others steered clear of him. They saw an annoying kid who looked different, talked too much, and couldn't stay sober. He didn't shower as much as everyone else, either. I would pick up Charlie from his halfway house in my rusty Plymouth Voyager minivan, with stickers shaped like bullet holes across its trunk, and take five more along with us. When we were all together in that van for the fifteen-minute commute to the Pioneer, there was unity, camaraderie, and a feeling of being a part of something. Priceless for people feeling alone in their world. I would know because I was Charlie, too; I had lived life on the outside for a long time.

***

Almost ten years earlier in Minneapolis, after Dad had died, I'd go days without eating during crack binges. When the hunger pains became overwhelming, I'd stake out the nearest McDonald's. Through the window, I'd watch families bounce in, laughing and eating together. The kids would get to playing on the indoor playground and leave behind their unfinished burgers. The mom would wrap it up and toss it into the nearest garbage can. Pacing, I'd wait for them to leave and then run inside to snatch it up. Three bites of a burger with a few dried-out fries smeared with ketchup. That was lunch. On a good day, they'd leave behind a few sips of soda, too.

One night, I stopped outside of Curly's Cafe on Lake Street, a twenty-four-hour restaurant where all the working girls would cram in to get out of the cold. I was broke—no money for food, no money for dope. I watched a cop pull into the Clark gas station next door and stumbled toward his passenger side door. Making sure he'd see me, I pissed on his door handle. I was begging to be arrested, for someone to take me out of there for a minute. They transferred me from the police station to the Mission Farms Detox

Center in Plymouth, a suburb of Minneapolis. For three days, I ate licorice and smoked rolled tobacco cigarettes. Free for the taking. There was even a lighter conveniently tied to a string on the counter for anyone to use. I had hot meals, a comfy bed, and warm showers. Got good enough to head right back out again with a bus coin in my pocket—a one-way ticket to the Twin Cities.

That summer, I was in and out of Mission Farms a dozen times. Enough to earn the nickname Frequent Flier. I'd even hitchhike down Highway 169 to get there just to escape the shelters for a few days. I bounced between Harbor Light, Catholic Charities, and an encampment next to Cedar Lake. Only when these places were full (and most of the time, they were), would I stare up at the Francis Drake Hotel with a pit in my stomach.

The Francis Drake was the roughest shelter I've ever experienced. Monotonously, I'd state my Social Security number and drag my feet up to a bed. In July, it was 87 degrees out, and I'd lie there, drenched in sweat on the third floor. All night long, mosquitoes buzzed relentlessly. Some mornings I would wake up and my shoes would be gone. I learned to zip them into my backpack, lock my arms through the straps, and sleep against it like a pillow. I followed the shadows of the wobbling ceiling fan that threatened to collapse any second. Eventually, the Francis Drake Hotel was shut down when a guard was shot out front.

I felt the extent of my fall when I was on a street corner. I was usually begging, "Hey, man, you got a dolla'? How 'bout you? You got one?" but not that day. I was just standing there when a sedan pulled up at the stop sign. I saw a woman with her young daughter in the passenger seat. The door lock clicked and she reached an arm over her child to roll up the window. My first instinct was to glance at the brick wall behind me and wonder,

"What is she worried about?" Then I realized she was protecting her kid from me, that she was scared of me. It was a punch to the stomach. I'd take a bullet to protect any woman and her child, even strangers. I'd never hurt them. But that's not what she saw.

I caught my reflection against a glass window and moved closer. I turned to my side and lifted my shirt a few inches. I probably only weighed a hundred pounds. I traced the deep grooves in my cheeks before pulling my lip up over my gums. I stared at the gaps where my teeth used to be, now littered with metal posts, and ran my finger over the jagged edge of a crooked tooth. When people asked me later if I had one wish, I would say, "I just want to be able to smile." I spent decades hiding my teeth behind a hand when I talked, or as I begged strangers for spare change.

I walked down Lake Street with twelve bucks in my pocket. Just eight short of a twenty rock. Behind me, I saw two shadows grow larger and larger. I was about to get jacked, and I wasn't even going to fight it. I never did. It was more like, "Here, just take my wallet," or I'd hide the little cash I had in my shoes under the sole. But they knew. They'd just take my shoes. Their footsteps quickened, closing in, when I heard a yell from the porch above me.

"Hey, man! That's White Boy Fred. Just leave 'im alone. He ain't nothing. He alright. Just leave 'im alone."

The two men pulled back, and when I looked up, I saw Oscar, a guy I sometimes smoked with who hung around the same places I did. In a fucked-up way, that moment made me feel like a part of something. Accepted. I had nothing else. My dad was dead, and I wasn't going to call Mom. Once a big-time chef who was now eating out of garbage cans. No, my shame ran too deep.

I imagined how a conversation with my family would go.

"Hey, Rory! How's it going?" *Shitty.*

"What are you up to?" *Nothing.*

"Are you working?" *No.*

"Where are you staying?" *Nowhere.*

I had nothing good to say, so why say anything? Not that I couldn't lie. I was quite good at that. When my probation officer would ask, "Hey, Rory, can you give us a clean UA?" I'd answer, "Sure! Absolutely! No problem. Anything you need." I knew I'd test positive from the coke I did the night before, but I'd respond without hesitating. Without a moment's pause to raise their suspicion, I could count on them to step back and follow up with, "Actually, you know what? We're good. We'll test you next time." I didn't want to go back to jail. At least not then. It had become a survival tactic to manipulate, cheat, and lie.

But I could never imagine lying to Mom and my brothers, anyone who I had respect for and loved. I'd already hurt Aunt Sylvia when I extorted money from her, and deep down, I didn't want to chip away at any last shred of integrity.

"How are you really doing?" I imagined them asking. *Well, I'm cold and hungry, living in a shelter, starving actually, failed at everything, let everyone down. I don't know, how are you doing?*

I feared that question, and if I didn't see them, they couldn't ask me, and I wouldn't have to lie.

Later, my brother, Tim, told me how he would spend weekends driving through Minneapolis, up and down the alleys and around shelters, looking for me without any luck. Cedar Lake was my usual place. I'd sit in the same spot in the woods for ten or twelve hours, completely still. Stuck. I didn't want to be found.

So when Oscar called out for me that night, I felt the same way a child does on Christmas morning, looking up at their mama and daddy, tearing off the gold wrapping from a present, with a fire crackling behind them. It was as good as it got. He had my back that night, and not much later, I had his.

Oscar and his girlfriend were in the business of robbing "Johns" together. She would lure men wearing wedding bands into hotel rooms while he hid in a closet. When the man was in a compromising position, Oscar would come out with a pistol and shove everything worth taking into a bag. No one ever called the police. What would they say? "Oh, I was trying to screw some woman behind my wife's back, and then…" It was the perfect crime, till one night it wasn't, and things went horribly wrong. A man refused to be robbed, and in the tussle, Oscar shot himself in the foot. Gangrene set in—red, blistery, and swollen, with the foulest smell. He called me in a panic, "Hey, Fred, you gotta get me outta here. I can't go to the ER anywhere around here, man. It's all over the news. My gun went off, and the guy snitched on me. As soon as I walk in, they'll know it was me."

At that point, Pony and G still had my car, in exchange for a forty rock every other day. I borrowed it back for a few days to drive Oscar across the border to a hospital in Wisconsin. As they started to wheel him inside, I called out for them to wait. I reached for the Stetson hat lying in the back seat, one of my only possessions. Whenever I finished a pack of cigarettes, I'd peel off the Marlboro miles from the side of the carton. When I collected enough, I'd leaf through the catalog and mail them in exchange for things like a backpack, a sweatshirt, and this hat. I smoothed it out and placed it in Oscar's hands. He cleared his throat and said, "You know, I never, ever liked a white guy." I was quick to reply, "I'm not white. I'm a fucking Jew, buddy." We laughed but we both felt the bond of friendship in our lonely worlds. He put the hat over his head and they wheeled him in. And back then, he didn't even know my real name.

***

So, when others didn't want to sponsor guys like Charlie or Shirtless Will, who would walk into the Pioneer Club naked from the waist up, or the Indian boy sleeping off a hangover in the back, or the homeless deaf guy who'd stumble in reeking of vodka…all those people no one "wanted," I was drawn to. When the AA leadership raised a pitchfork against Shirtless Will and were ready to kick him out, I attended the board meetings and stood up for him.

"The only requirement to be here is a desire to quit drinking. I'm sorry if you don't like him. But we can't push him out. We have to love him. Fuck, we have to love him more. Think about it. Because he's more fucked-up than us. We can't turn our backs on him because he won't wear his fucking shirt. Instead of yelling at him, let's take him aside and calmly talk to him. 'Will, this is a problem, man.'"

When I was finished, Mark, who was often the first to cast stones, reminded members to meet up on Tuesday for a final decision about Will. I'd helped Mark pack up and move twice now, and in private, I said, "I need a huge favor from you, man. I've never asked you for one, so this is a big deal. Can you help me out?"

"Yeah, Rory. Anything."

"Good, because it's going to be a hard one. You see, there's this guy—Will." Mark raised his eyebrows and gave me a quick look before turning his eyes toward his shoes. "Since I can't be here on Tuesday, and there's so much commotion about kicking Will out, can you help me out and stand up for him? He's our brother. Everyone deserves our love. And the people who need it most, we've got to love them the hardest. We've had talks about that before and agreed on that, no matter what someone does. I know he's kinda mouthy, fights against the grain. I realize that, but can you do me a favor and stand up for him?" With one last effort, I slapped my palms together and begged. "Because he's still a fucking human being."

I didn't know how much he heard till two weeks later. Mark walked over and said, "You fucker. What you said, that changed me." I didn't react right away; I didn't want him to see me, so I got into my car, laid my head against the steering wheel, and wept. Mark was a sword-thrower, and I got him to listen and change his mind. My words mattered, and that meant everything to me.

Will got to stay. After a while, he even started wearing a shirt to meetings, though he'd pull it off as soon as he left the Pioneer.

I didn't want to sponsor the guy in treatment whose mommy and daddy would visit every week with a carton of cigarettes. I wanted to walk up to the dude who came off the block dirty, sat in the back, still reeking of alcohol, and ask him, "Hey, do you want a cup of coffee?" I wanted the hard cases, and when they climbed into my truck, I'd just hold my breath. One guy, who was kicked out of every bar in town, pissed his pants in the front seat. I got a rag and cleaner, and we drove on.

When I had almost two years of AA meetings under my belt, I tacked a handwritten note on the community bulletin board: "Need a ride to St. Paul. Will pay for gas with an extra $20." I heard a deep, gravely voice behind me ask, "What day you need to go?" It was Indian Mike. He hung around the Pioneer Club and was usually outside as he smoked two packs a day. He was quiet, always watching—a gentle face beneath a severe expression—and when he spoke, we all stopped to listen. He had the kind of voice you could hear in a crowd, not because it was loud, but because it would always find its place.

I told him that I had to be there on Tuesday to show all of my signed ducks in a row and finally get my driver's license back after three DUIs. He'd drive on one condition—that we stop at the casino on the way back. The day of, I climbed into his old beat-up Chevy Blazer with windows that wouldn't roll all the way up. We were frozen by the time we arrived. I grabbed my envelope stuffed with documents that I'd attended the required recovery meetings, along with letters from my probation officer and others who could testify to my character.

When I walked into the transportation department, I heard someone shout, "Hey, Fred! Hey, Fred!" I'd practically forgotten my nickname from the streets and ignored him. But the guy kept on till I heard, "Yes, you! White Boy Fred!" It was Oscar. "Oh, man, I knew that was you with your funky-ass walk! It's Rory now? Well, you look good. Damn, you look good. You come up. I'll tell you, I found Jesus. And that's my wife right there. And we go to church each week." Words poured from him as he tried fitting in the years of strength spent turning his life around into sixty seconds. When we said goodbye, he whispered, "You know, you still the only white man that I ever liked. You the only one. Man, you had my back when I needed ya. I told my wife the stories a hundred times. I can't believe you're standing right here! And let me tell you, I still got your hat, man."

After that, Indian Mike drove straight to Treasure Island as he'd wanted. And six hours later, we were still there. That was his place to socialize, to smoke his cigarettes, to talk to people he knew... home. Like AA had become for me.

Three weeks later, I got a letter stating my driver's license had officially been reinstated.

IF YOU WEREN'T THINKING
ABOUT YOURSELF SO MUCH,
MAYBE THINGS WOULDN'T
BE SO BAD

Thanksgiving was coming up, and I called Indian Mike, who'd taken over as my sponsor when Glen passed away. Around the holidays, I often thought of Mom. How, after one too many mimosas, she'd feel inspired and buy a large batch of king crab and shrimp and host a crab boil. A couple times a year, we'd warm ourselves against the bubbling pot and share funny stories, like the time Mom sent my brother, Tim, and me to pick raspberries near our weekend cabin. There were rows and rows of bushes, all taller than me. Tim and I were popping berries into our mouths and filling our buckets when we suddenly heard pounding feet and a deep growl. We screamed and ran for our lives, dropping a trail of berries behind us. When we finally looked back, we saw Grandpa chasing us with his arms stretched over his head. Mom had set us up.

She would cook an extravagant roasted turkey dinner with all the trimmings every year. A creamy green bean casserole, mashed potatoes, and a homemade cranberry sauce. On Thanksgiving, my brothers and I would declare a temporary ceasefire on the hair-pulling, flicking, and kicking under the table. Grandma and Grandpa would join us. These nights were special because they were rare.

Once I started Hebrew school, my days were long. After finishing my regular classes at public school, I'd hop on a second bus that would bring me to Talmud Torah in Saint Louis Park. On weeknights, I wouldn't see home again till after 9:30 p.m., when everyone was already asleep. This was my routine for four years, all the way till high school. Every night, when I opened the fridge, there was a plate covered with plastic wrap waiting for me. I'd turn on a small light, drag a single chair from the kitchen counter, and pull back the plastic. After eating alone night after night, even during the summer, those large family dinners meant everything.

Over the phone, I explained to Indian Mike how the holidays were a reminder that I'd been such a good kid who turned into such a disappointment. There was a time when I would go to bars just to wait for someone to tell me, "My dad died," so I could snicker, "Dude, shut up. Both my parents are dead. Oh, and my best friend from when I was a kid OD'd. Why don't you buy *me* a drink, huh? I don't want to hear your shit." Or, "Your wife left you? Who cares? At least you had one to leave you. What are you crying about?" Even the bartender would slap free Bacardi Cokes in front of me. I knew my mom and dad had still seen everything I'd done, from wherever they were, and that killed me.

I bared it all to Indian Mike, trusting my sponsor, trying to bond with him. There was a long pause on the other end. Then Indian Mike finally barked out, "You know, Rory, if you weren't thinking about yourself so much, maybe things wouldn't be so bad. And if you're looking for sympathy, go find someone else because I've used all mine up on myself." And he hung up. That fucking . asshole.

Enraged, I dialed him back. "That came from my heart, man! What's wrong with you? I'm sharing some personal shit about my family, and you're going to say that?"

He stayed steady. "I guess you didn't hear me the first time. If you weren't thinking about yourself so much, maybe things wouldn't seem so bad." *Click.*

I rarely opened up to anyone, and this guy was just tearing me down. I was ready to kick his ass right back. I stewed and paced, but by the time I called him a third time, I was calmer. I knew he was trying to make a point. He always was.

"Just tell me what you're trying to say."

"I've been listening to the radio, Rory. Looks like the Salvation Army is short on food this year. You sit at the AA club and go on and on about how all these people helped you, how you slept in shelters when you had nothing. You used to be a chef, right? So why don't you go make something? Why don't you go fucking do something for them and quit whining and thinking about yourself so much?"

That night in bed, my thoughts drifted back to one particular Thanksgiving at the Dorothy Day shelter. Churches in town had come together to bring us a turkey buffet dinner with all the fixings and platters of fruit. I scooped up pieces of pineapple onto my plate and took a seat at a plastic folding table. It was the sweetest, juiciest, freshest fruit I'd ever tasted, everything a piece of fruit could be. That taste sunk so deep I've never forgotten it.

The next day, I drove to Cub Foods and bought enough fruit for five trays. I'd served VIP guests in hotels before and could carve a swan from an apple. I laid down a bed of lettuce, delicately arranged the assortment of fruit on top, and sprinkled in Andes chocolates with the mint-green wrap. I called Indian Mike as I drove across town to churches and shelters.

I heard him say, "Looks like you fucking listened to me. Bet you stopped feeling sorry for yourself, didn't ya?"

That asshole saved my life. I've delivered fruit trays at Thanksgiving every year since to the Dorothy Day House, the Ronald McDonald House, the Cronin Home, Pathways, the Pioneer Club…all the places around Rochester that helped me. Sometimes, I'll receive a card with a handwritten thank-you note. Most people lock up jewels in their home safes; I keep those cards in mine.

I waited a long time to pull an Indian Mike on someone else, and I got my chance when I was sponsoring Steve, who was now off of house arrest. He called me again to complain.

"Dude, my son's in South Dakota with my ex. The roads are covered in snow and they just shut down I-90. I can't get there, man."

It sounded like Steve was going to be alone on Christmas and was feeling sorry for himself. But I wouldn't allow that. "Well," I began, "if you weren't thinking about yourself so much, maybe things wouldn't be so bad."

Click.

I did a little dance on my side of the phone. I'd been waiting fucking years to do that.

And when Steve called back cursing, I interrupted, "Maybe you're not hearing me right. If you didn't think about yourself so much, maybe it wouldn't bother you so bad."

The second time felt just as good.

When he called a third time, I got straight to the point. "Steve, I've been hearing on the radio that the Salvation Army is short on bell ringers this year. Maybe you can ring a bell at one of these places. Why don't you do that? If you find a place, I'll come ring with you. You can get out and do something for others, or you can just sit there and feel sorry for yourself." For three straight days leading up to Christmas, he signed himself up for eight-hour shifts at Walmart North. As with most of us in recovery, it was often "go big or go home" for us. I think it's because, deep down, we know all the horrible shit we've done, so when we get a chance to do something good, we're all in.

There were eight of us AA guys who joined Steve, broken men from off the street, ringing bells and belting out holiday songs. We held up traffic with our signs and megaphones. "Noel, Noeeeeel!" We were terrible enough to get a crowd around us, laughing, clapping, and begging us to stop singing while throwing in twenties. We collected so many donations we had to call the Salvation Army twice to come around and empty the overflowing bucket. Two cops showed up to direct traffic, and later, a news crew rolled in to get footage.

Steve and I weren't the only ones who've felt alone on Christmas. It's common in recovery to feel like crap when the holidays come around; we can't find joy because our family's gone and there's no one left to gather around the tree. And every holiday party serves up alcohol. So there we were in subzero weather, ringing bells. The next year, we came in costume, and bell ringing became an annual tradition for the next five years.

Whenever I hear the guys I sponsor vent about judges and probation officers and exes, I interrupt and ask them to circle up. "Alright, it's morning time! We're going to do our daily meditation. Everyone, together now. Let's sing, 'Me-me-me-me-meeeeeeeee!'" With my highest pitch, I'll drag out the last note till I get chuckles out of them.

"But that's what you do, right? You wake up, and right away, you think all about yourself—'me-me-me-me-meeeee!' You make all your plans, and when they fail throughout the day, when people say or do things you don't want, now you're a pissed-off, miserable, unhappy person. Well, this isn't my world or yours. You only have a choice in how you receive this world, in how you respond. When you get let down, you have a bad day. How's that working for you? Instead, how about you take a step back and don't put so much expectation on everything? Then your feelings might not get hurt so much. And maybe you'll stay sober."

I knew the real reason Steve was so upset when he called from his car that snowy day. He was a year sober and wanted to show off to his whole family how well he was doing and how much his life had changed. But the entire time he was ringing bells, he couldn't sit around and stew about his plans and designs not working out. When he got out of his head and into the world, things didn't seem so bad.

I've had my own moments of struggling with the unexpected. Most recently, when finding out about my stage IV lung cancer. After hearing my diagnosis, I wanted to shout back, "Who the fuck do you think I am? Look at everything I've been through. How do you think I can handle this?" Doctors suggested palliative care, where patients with serious illnesses manage their pain and create a care plan to improve their quality of life. In my mind, it might as well have been called the "End of Life" department.

I'd just started sponsoring my old friend, Dale, and decided to bring him with me to a chemotherapy appointment. This was a maneuver, but it wasn't a "poor me" move. No, like Indian Mike, I could feel sorry for myself enough on my own. I didn't need that from anyone else. Even as I talked with Dale—this guy who towered over me with bulging muscles built up in prison and tattoos covering his arms—I could see how broken he felt, how consumed his mind was. I could almost hear his thoughts drowning him, thoughts of his recent divorce and having to sell his house.

But buddy, you're not sick.

I didn't use those words. But taking him to this appointment was me trying to show him.

Dale had isolated himself, trying to manage things as an "I," alone. We hadn't had a meaningful interaction in a long time, but when I'd learned something was going on in his personal life and he wasn't answering my calls, I made a couple of laps around his house, peeking through his windows. I must have tripped his security camera on his cell because my phone rang. He shouted, "What are you doing out there? *What do you want?*" I told him, "Relax, bro. I'm worried about you."

It turned out, he wasn't sitting around in the dark thinking about smoking coke or meth after twenty years. It was more destructive than that. He'd been planning on boarding a plane, walking out to the desert, and never coming back.

I brought him with me that day out of love. I could give pep talks till I was blue in the face, but these three hours in the Mayo building would let him breathe for a moment. I knew he was going through hell, and it sucked, but maybe he would see that it could be worse, that he still had people around who loved him. That eventually he'd be okay with those people in his corner. For three hours, I knew he wouldn't be thinking about his shit. Maybe instead he would see that he was part of a "we." With the chemo drugs pumping through my veins, with Dale at my bedside, I hoped I'd remember, too.

WHAT'S YOUR HEART SAYING YOU SHOULD DO?

In 2003, when I was two full years sober after the SA Bandit stint in jail, I parked my bike at Rob's Construction and Kenny approached me. "Rory, you're the best employee we've got. Never missed a day, never been late. You're always here." He didn't know how much I feared downtime. It would take one free minute and a bit of cash in my pocket and I'd be off, chasing a hit.

He paused before continuing, "But listen, you need to take some time off for yourself. My wife and I love you and want to thank you, so we're sending you to Mexico, buddy. Last year, we stayed in Cancún at an amazing hotel called the Melia Turqesa. It's right on this beautiful white-sand beach with a view of the Caribbean. You're gonna love it, Rory. It's all-inclusive, and we'll pay for everything. Just go and enjoy yourself."

I counted the days till I boarded the plane, excited about the seven days ahead in a country I'd never been before. On my way to the hotel after landing, I stopped at a flea market with T-shirts and little souvenirs. People were eager to sell me personally engraved rice grains and small "Cancún, Mexico" magnets when

I walked through the door. I made my way through the chaos and saw a set of stairs removed from the rest of the market. I liked the quiet. I followed the steps up to a room with glass walls lined with boxes of cigars and grabbed a couple to smoke later. Here I was in Mexico, cigars in hand, picking out souvenirs for my sponsor and buddies back at the Pioneer Club. Life was good, and I was smiling.

The next thing I knew, the guy behind the counter pulled out a tray: cocaine, marijuana, meth, ecstasy, crack. A fucking buffet. He'd read me the moment I walked in and was persistent. "I hook you up. What you want? I give you good deal."

Oh, boy. I remember pausing long enough to make the guy nervous. "What you want, huh? So you want something or no?" He didn't know the battle raging in my mind. *I'm doing so well right now. Sober, holding down a job, just got my license back... Come on, Rory. Don't. No!*

But that's not what I said. "Give me a twenty rock."

I raced to the resort and rode the glass elevator straight to my room. I crushed a can, sprinkled some cigarette ash on top, broke off a piece of crack and lit it. To this day, it was the best cocaine I have ever smoked. With that first hit, with that one little taste, I knew I was going to die in Mexico. When I blew it out, everything I'd missed for the past two years came rushing back. Things weren't going to end well. There was a whole tray out there, and I had cash. It was a dream of mine to go deep-sea fishing and catch a blue marlin or sailfish. I'd saved up and brought an extra two thousand dollars to have one stuffed to bring home with me. But the cocaine in Mexico was cheap. The choice was made for me.

I snaked my way back through the flea market and brought back an ounce of coke this time. An ounce was what dealers would break up to sell in grams or quarter ounces to everyone else. I bought the whole damn thing. My fingers were so shaky that I had to rest the spoon handle over the edge of the nightstand and use a heavy lamp base to hold it steady. I gripped the lighter with both hands till it flickered under the spoon. I watched the coke break down as it cooked, and it was the clearest I'd ever seen.

Here I was, sitting in front of the best crack cocaine with no one around to bother me. A drug addict's fantasy. I was in a different country, so I knew if I got caught, I'd get thrown in jail and disappear. No mama or daddy to call. But I didn't care because I believed that, after three or four hits, as strong as they were, I would have a heart attack and die right there on the bathroom floor anyway. I gave in to the thought: this was it, and I was prepared. It wasn't that my life back home was so bad; the addiction was just too strong. With every puff, my heart pounded harder through my chest. My lips were numb. I'd smoked crack most of my life, buying it off the block, but this was a different level of peace. I was screwed.

The next seven days were a blur of taxi cabs to and from dealers and strip clubs. I even got high on the road with a cab driver when he offered his stash and said, "This is the good stuff right here." From the back seat, I traded him coke for PCP or maybe it was heroin. Ironically, I thought I was being slick and safe by making him try the stuff he was giving me first. I was in a different country, after all. "C'mon," he said afterward. "I'll take you to the good place. Where the good girls are."

The next morning, I somehow remembered it was the day I had to catch a plane home. I stumbled into a cab and when we arrived at the airport, I grabbed my suitcase from the trunk, slammed it shut, and stood there. I still had about a thousand bucks left. I looked around and muttered, "Fuck this." I called out to the driver and got a room at a hotel a few doors down from the Melia Turqesa and bought a lobster dinner to take back to my room. I didn't even know if I'd eaten anything in the last five days. I took a hit with one hand and broke off a piece of lobster tail with the other.

Kenny had given me a company credit card. I charged two more nights before he froze the account. He'd been worried ever since my plane landed and I was a no-show in Minneapolis. When I finally called him back days later, he shouted in my ear, "Holy shit! What'd you do? We called the Melia Turqesa and they've got the police looking for you?! They're saying you stole a pack of cigarettes?"

At the resort, I was going down to the lobby shop all the time and charging things to my room. On my last day there, I took a pack of smokes, but the lady grabbed them from my hands and said no. I barked out, "Just charge it!" Still no. She must have guessed that I'd bail before paying the bill. I snatched the carton back, hard this time, and I must have hit her shoulder when I did. In Mexico, or anywhere else for that matter, you don't push or grab a woman and take things from her. Kenny listened as I finally admitted that I'd relapsed. After a long silence, he said with disbelief, "So you're on the run now and fucking high in Mexico? Jesus."

I still had some cash left on me. I dragged my little rollaway suitcase behind me and called for a cab. The driver took me to the old downtown part of Cancún, the real Mexico where the locals live. I got a cheap room, a tight space where the ceiling fan wobbled fast above me. I roasted in the heat, got wasted on crack, and blacked out. When I heard a series of loud knocks, I stumbled toward the door. It was the Federales, the Mexican police. They'd caught up to me.

They shoved me into a police truck and dragged me across a dirt floor with a hole to shit and piss in. Maggots feasted inside it. In all the jails I'd been to, I got to work out in a gym, wear freshly laundered clothes, and could count on a tray full of hot food every day. But I was far from home. *Am I ever going to learn?* I wondered. *This is bad. I could disappear today.* News reached Kenny who made some calls on my behalf.

Finally, they worked out a deal. I had to get on a plane, get the hell out of Mexico, and never come back. An airline representative and an American consulate in Mexico stood on either side of me when we got to the airport. The Federales surrounded us in their green trucks, and I heard one of them say I wasn't ever welcome back and to never step foot on their soil again. I muttered, "Well, I didn't fucking like it here anyhow. Fuck you." The American consulate elbowed me hard in the ribs and hissed, "Shut your fucking mouth and get on the plane. Don't you understand? Get out of here."

When I landed in Minneapolis, I got down to my knees and kissed the ground. Kenny pulled up in his Escalade, and I climbed into the front seat. When he finally turned to me, he jumped back. "Jesus Christ! Did you even eat while you were over there?!" It was supposed to be a seven-day, fun-filled vacation, yet here I was, thirteen days later, coming off of a crack cocaine run.

Miraculously, Kenny kept me on. Rob of Rob's Construction had died and left behind a little house that I now rented from Kenny. I'd stay clean for a few days, only to take a hit while on a break from painting trim. This went on for a year before I vowed to get sober again, but that was yet another broken promise. I knew Kenny would have done anything to help me, both he and his wife, but my shame was too much.

I walked away from the house and couch-hopped around town, getting high. When a neighbor watched in horror as I ran around the living room in boxers and stopped at the window to dance, I just moved onto the next couch. One of my only possessions left was the motorcycle I'd drive to Chester Woods Park to smoke in peace. When I dropped my last hit in the trees one night, I crawled around for hours looking for it. It wasn't long before I sold that bike to a salesman at Rob's and took the money straight to a dealer.

Rachel, my probation officer, knew my habit of smoking crack in cheap motels anytime I had enough cash saved up. I figured if I was getting high alone, I couldn't hurt anyone. I wouldn't do that to my buddies and their families. She handed out flyers with my picture to all the local motels along Broadway, looking for me. I kept my hood up and tightened it around my face when I checked into a room one night. As soon as I came off a hit, I called Kenny.

I heard him say sadly, "God, Rory. Aren't you getting tired of this life? In and out of motels all the time?"

Yes, I was so tired. *I didn't know what life I wanted, but I knew it wasn't this.* That same night, I walked past the fairgrounds to the government center. I swiped a cigarette butt from the ashtray, and as I started to light it, I heard a guard's voice from behind. "We've been waiting for you."

I turned myself in for violating probation.

I was sentenced to sixty days, a mandatory treatment program with a urine test twice a day, and weekly AA meetings. I sat in jail waiting for a treatment bed and heard other inmates spew out, "Why did this happen to me? I have the worst goddamn luck!" But I didn't say a fucking word. I gotta do time? Yep. Because I'd messed up. I could lie to everyone else, but I had to get right with myself. Inside, I screamed, *What do I want? Do I want to die alone and miserable?*

In jails, I'd read *National Geographic* and learn about exotic places around the world. Little huts sitting over crystal-clear waters. The magazines were hot commodities for their photographs of women in traditional clothing with their breasts hanging out. Some of the inmates even had cutouts dangling over their beds. Topless Polynesian women. (I don't know how the jailers never caught on.) I turned the pages to remote beaches, soaking up articles about snorkeling through coral reefs and gliding through a school of rainbow-colored fish. It was like reading a romance novel; I was so emotionally invested that I could almost smell the salty ocean mist.

But when I closed the cover, harsh reality came crashing down—I was still locked up in jail. And once my time was up, I had nowhere to go. There was no mama or daddy anymore, waiting to pick me up. With the weight of that, I dropped to the floor and curled up.

My happiest times were when I smoked crack alone, getting "stuck" with no one else around. I would look at that piece of rock, that next hit, and wonder, *How much do I have left? What time is it? Do I have enough money to get more?* I'd spent nearly two decades of my life feeding my addiction, chasing the pleasure that would run through me, and hating myself for it. I spent all my energy searching for it. Stuck on it. Consumed by it.

How many times had I thought, *I don't know what I want, but it isn't this?* All those moments flooded back.

That Thanksgiving day, eating an expired turkey sandwich on a gas station curb, alone.

Driving back from Warrington, Florida, with a black eye instead of the rock I'd paid for, alone.

Wandering the streets of Minneapolis—too ashamed to get near any family—alone.

Stuck in a cycle of treatment centers and relapses. Alone.

The question still hung in the air: *What did I want then?*

I buried my face in my hands, trying to stop the flow of tears. From deep within, my longing for companionship broke through. What I wanted was to love and be loved back, something crack could never give me. But I was living my life in a way that made this impossible—alone. To have any hope of having a partner and bonding with people, I couldn't use. Maybe others could, but I couldn't, not with how my body reacts. I had to be 100 percent sober for a chance at joy and a good life. And if I was going to use, I might as well go back to Mexico and get across the border somehow. But I'd tried to stop so many times before and felt trapped.

Sobs coursed through me and I imagined myself hanging from a bedsheet noose tied to the jail cell bars. I didn't want to keep living this way, but I couldn't change either. And if I couldn't stop, then fuck it.

Wake up, Rory! Do I want to fucking live or not?

I choked back a sob and the dark image skipped to another: A nice house, not big, just mine, maybe with a fresh coat of paint. Inside, I could feel the warmth of a healthy relationship with another human being. Then I saw an ocean lined with white quartz sands.

I had to try. I'd written my first two failed sobriety dates into the inside cover of my copy of *Alcoholics Anonymous*: *March 20, 2001* (the night of the SA Bandit charge) and *June 4, 2004* (a year after Mexico). This time, I wrote *August 18, 2005*—my last and final sobriety date—on the inside of the *back* cover. I'd tried to quit so many times before; I was ready to do things differently this time.

I had turned my back on my Jewish faith out of shame. With what little spirituality still lingered inside of me, I found a higher power of *my own understanding* to sustain me, right there on that jail cell floor. I was just so tired—wanting to change but unable to; stuck in a vicious, drug-riddled cycle. In the past, I'd say things like, "If only I were with her, things would be good," or, "If only I had a better job, everything would be fine." Well, I got the job and she came back, but I was still getting fucking high. So that wasn't it. Alone, I would stay sober for a while, but when I fell, it was too comfortable and easy to just lie there. How many times had that happened already? I'd lost count.

I needed a power greater than myself that I could rely on to help me avoid and resist the temptation of crack and alcohol. A power that would guide me away from the nearest bar, provide a safety net if I fell, and be the push of motivation to keep moving forward, one day at a time.

Today, I know that wherever I go and whatever I do, even if I make a mistake, even if I start using again and lose everything, even if I have to die with this cancer inside of me, that my God has my back. He may not be your God or their God, but He's *my* God as I understand Him, and He's fucking right there with me; I'll never have to go through anything by myself again.

To have that comfort, as someone who has lost so much and been ashamed for so long, as someone who has lived on the streets and in the woods alone, my relying on whatever that is, whatever we call it, is what fucking saved my life.

***

In the years after my release, I still wanted to sponsor the hard cases. That never changed.

I scooted next to the twenty-something Indian boy who was sitting alone in the back of the Pioneer Club one night. He was wearing a winter hat that was too small for his head. All around me, I heard, "Ah, he don't ever stay sober. He's just going to ask for money." And he did.

"Hey, man, you got a dollar? You got a square?"

"No, I don't, but I can give you some work. Meet me tomorrow, early, and you can get all the cigarettes you want." My tactic was always a 6 a.m. call because half of them wouldn't show up. Most could get up and walk uphill there and back in a foot of snow to a liquor store, but they couldn't get up and fucking meet me? Well, then they weren't ready.

But, the next morning, the boy shuffled in. He took off his hat, shook his shaggy black hair, and let out the long breath he'd been holding. His name was Jeremiah (Miah, as I know my friend today). With his one bag and a backpack, he'd been sleeping in the skyways connecting the Mayo Clinic buildings. Sometimes, he'd wander into the Marriott downtown and sleep upright on their lobby couch. Whenever he heard footsteps approach, he'd quickly open his eyes and act like he was sitting there like anyone else. When Miah was fourteen, his uncle had poured him a mix of Kahlua and coconut rum on Christmas night and a switch flipped on inside. Almost ten years later, here we were.

He confided, "You know, when you're young, you never imagine this is where the road will end...at the bottom. I still remember the first time I saw you speak at a meeting when I was just sixteen. I was the youngest one there, just sitting and thinking, 'What kind of a stupid story is this? It ain't got nothing to do with me. I've never done anything like that, never drank a whole bottle before.' But now I get it, how all that stuff will come if you keep on keeping on. I'm here now because all these years later, you're still sober and working and happy. That's all I want."

"There's still a lot of road left," I said, handing him a copy of *Alcoholics Anonymous*. "I want you to read up to this page I marked and then meet me back here at 1 p.m. tomorrow." As we worked through the steps, he paused at all the mentions of God. He agreed he was powerless over alcohol, how it made his life unmanageable, how he had tried to quit on his own but couldn't. The steps ask that we turn to a power greater than ourselves to support us, to "God as we understood Him."

With all the men I've worked with over the years, I've stepped inside the Buddhist Temple off of Marion Road, churches of all kinds (Lutheran, Catholic, Presbyterian), and synagogues too. Once, a young Somali man with a wooden eye took me to the mosque on Broadway Avenue and I met his parents. My Native American friends would share about the Great Spirit. In each of these places—whether singing in church or standing by a river watching Natives dance in their grand powwow regalia—I'd feel chills run down me. To me, they've all got something going on.

"But I don't pray," Miah told me. "If I do, I'll get something I don't really want. If I pray for strength, I'll get hit by a bus or something to build up my strength. If I pray for patience, I'll hit every red light. But I've always liked eagles, seeing their beauty and how they fly the way they do."

"Well, that's spiritual thinking right there," I said. "Maybe watching those eagles makes you reach for something higher, too."

I tell the guys I work with that when they think about their higher power, they should feel hopeful. I remember when Steve was trying to get sober, he'd complain about other people's success and how he got nothing but failure. I wanted to understand him.

"What are your feelings about God?" I asked.

He rattled off all the reasons he thought God was unfair, how he didn't believe in God, how God never—

"Hold on a second," I interrupted him. "Let's think about this. If you think God is unfair and not being nice to you, and that you don't have it as good as everybody else, then you think there is a God, right? So why don't you turn that belief into a God that's good for you?"

I instructed Steve like I do the other guys I sponsor, telling them to grab a pencil and a little piece of paper—it needs to be little so they can carry it with them. "I want you to describe your God to me. I know my God by looking at my life and rewinding the camera. I know He's forgiving because I've been a fucking asshole and I'm still sitting here today. I know He's loving. I know He's understanding because it takes a lot to tolerate me. I know He's caring. I know He's accepting. You don't have to write fifty things."

Later, when these guys call me and complain, "I'm having the worst day ever. I don't know what to do. My wife is talking about leaving me… I hate my boss… I'm in trouble… It's fucking raining… I didn't get the day off… I stubbed my toe…" I'll tell them, "You know what to do."

"What do you mean?"

"Why don't you pull that piece of paper out? You said your boss said no to a raise and you don't know what to do? I'm sure something on that paper will be your answer. If that's who you think your God is, and if your God could talk to you, wouldn't He want you to be this way too? Wouldn't He want you to be loving, caring, kind, forgiving, accepting?"

"Well, yeah."

"So, if you can look me in the eye and tell me you really believe that if your higher power, whoever it is, whatever it is, had a voice and words, that that's what they would say to do…well, that's your answer right there. It's not about whether you think it's a good idea or the right idea. Your boss didn't give you the raise you asked for, but you say you like your job? Try being understanding and fucking patient. You already know what to do."

Click. I'd pull an Indian Mike and hang up.

Human beings are reactors, and that can be our biggest downfall. Indian Mike would say, "We make decisions with our head, our dick, or our wallet. How about we start making decisions with this?" and he'd tap his chest. That piece of paper with the things we say we value is the pause between thought and action. What should I do here? What's in my control? What should I let go of? I'm winging life a lot of the time, but even if I fuck up, it doesn't matter because I went with my heart and I'm okay with it. I'd rather have nothing and feel good than have everything and feel shitty. Pretty easy.

When Steve started accepting that doing things alone the way he always had was giving him the same results, hangover after hangover, I left him with a reminder: "Just turn the handle on the door so when you have to go crashing through it, it's not latched."

One afternoon, Steve was alone in the kitchenette of his one-bedroom basement apartment. He had a mini fridge, a hot plate, and a single window for company. While making a sandwich, he dropped a bottle of mayonnaise. As glass shattered across the floor, his anger exploded. He swept an arm across the counter, more jars and knives and plates falling to the floor. He threw his bottle against the window, cracking both. Wrenching open his cupboards, he smashed their contents to the ground too. Then he cried and screamed and dropped to his knees, shards of glass digging into him. It may have been five minutes or five hours, he couldn't say. His dog ran into the closet, scared, as Steve begged, "God, if you can take this over, take it over. I can't do this no more. I don't know how to live with drugs, and I can't live without them. So I just don't want to live."

He had partied every night, and for the past sixteen years, drugs and alcohol were involved in some part of his day. Going without either seemed impossible. Only when he was ready to rely on something other than himself for an answer did that belief turn the door handle. And when Steve crashed, he crashed through an opening of hope.

To this day, I stay connected to something stronger than me—something spiritual, a kind of spirit guide. The closer it is, the better shot I have of not turning to crack if I'm near Dale Street or after an argument with a difficult subcontractor or inside a Mexican flea market again. Me and my own will? History has shown I'm a reactor, and I won't fare well. I tell the guys I sponsor to find something that lifts them, whether that's a version of a religious God or the power of a community that has struggled with the same problem. Maybe it's the feeling inside you when you see beams of sunlight falling through the clouds on your drive home, or maybe a soulful melody that transports you. Miah has his eagles. And I'm reminded of that power every time I stand under the stars at night, in awe...

We're all a part of a greater whole.

A few of Rory's mugshots leading up to his arrest on August 18, 2005, his last and final sobriety date

PULL BACK YOUR HOOD AND *BE A PART OF. SAY YES.*

Back in 2001, after my third DUI, when I first came to Rochester for treatment, the counselor at the Pathway House praised me midway through the program. "You're staying sober and showing up every day for work at the Kahler. We see how good you're doing."

Like at Levee's Cafe before, the head chef at the Kahler Grand Hotel had looked through my experience in the culinary world and skeptically asked, "You absolutely sure you want to flip eggs? Then we'll take you for as long as we can get you. One question: can you carve?" On Mother's Day, they put me in the dining room with a coat and tie as the rest of the staff glared at the new kid, center stage.

The counselor leaned forward and continued, "As part of your recovery, we strongly recommend you volunteer somewhere. There's the Dorothy Day shelter, or you can help serve food at the church, or—"

"What's the closest place you've got?" I interrupted. With three DUIs, I had to walk or ride my bike to go anywhere.

The next day, I stopped at the Ronald McDonald House, a home away from home for families coming to Mayo for medical appointments. I filled out an informational sheet. *Have you ever been convicted of a crime?* I checked the boxes truthfully. On Friday nights, I took out the garbage, bottled up bags of donated metal caps, and did other small jobs that needed to be taken care of. When I felt the itch to start a conversation, I'd tell myself, "Don't ask nobody nothing. Not how they're doing or where they're from. Head down, Rory." As I swept the floor, I watched the same older couple walk in each week to read stories to the kids. When they didn't show one night, I was asked to take over. Sure, I could give it a shot.

I took in the kids' curious faces on me in anticipation. I sat up front like I'd seen my teachers do, held the book high, and mechanically turned the pages. When I finished reading, they politely clapped their little hands. I was invited back as a regular reader between my cleaning duties but they gave me some advice. "The kids like big gestures and different voices for characters. If you're excited, they'll get excited, so find the right books and they'll love it, you know?"

No, I *didn't* know. What they saw was the clean-cut Rory standing in front of them, not the crack addict who had nothing to offer nobody. I walked to the Rochester Public Library down the street and told a couple of librarians what I'd been tasked to do. A little old lady came back with an armful of books. "So we picked these out for the kids. This one's about a train going up a hill. It has a lot of action. The kids will love it. And this one is…" I listened, gratefully nodded, and brought the stack with me to the Ronald McDonald House the next Friday.

As I restocked the fridge with bread and milk, I saw moms holding their little ones. With my finely honed crackhead hearing skills, I caught bits and pieces of their hushed conversations. "It's alright, Mommy. I'm okay." People had said to me, "It could always be worse," but watching how much worse it could be with my own eyes? That sunk deep. I'd been walking around with shame for so long, my head hung low, consumed by self-pity, but these mamas and their kids checked me. Shut your mouth and get back up. That night, I made the books come alive. I was a thirty-year-old standing on chairs, knocking things over at the right moments. The kids just laughed, and their parents did too.

I emerged from the shadows; between my job as a breakfast cook at the Kahler and going to meetings and now volunteering, I was becoming a part of society again. On Thursdays, when I walked into the library with an empty bag, it was like I was famous. "Hey, it's Rory! Rory's here!" Of course, there were rules, so it was more of an excited whisper. And on Fridays, when the kids caught sight of me, they would chant my name. I was their hero, but really, they were mine.

One Friday, I saw the parents but not their kid. The mom walked toward me, her steps heavy. "Rory, Sandra didn't make it. We wanted you to know how much she'd talk about you in her last days, how funny she thought you were. You brought her so much joy." Fuck, did that affect me. Still does. I was just starting to learn how to be okay in my own skin again, that my words and craziness could actually help others. And all I was doing was reading a book. She said with a hug, "We just wanted to say thank you."

The next Friday, I walked in as I always did, but the gal stopped me at the desk. "Listen, Rory. We don't know how to tell you this, but we realized you've got a criminal record. We have vulnerable clients here as you know. We're so sorry, but you can't be here anymore."

With that, everything came crashing down. The first of anything good that I'd done in a long time...pulled from under me. When a buddy mentioned his regular spot for getting coke behind a downtown bar, it became mine too. For a few months, anyway—till I robbed the SuperAmerica.

***

Five years later, after my spiritual awakening on the jail cell floor, I knew if I got back on crack that I'd be back on the streets. How long would I stay trapped in the cycle? I committed to staying sober but was hunched over again with the weight of all the shit I'd done since Mexico, all for a hit of a white powder and the rush I'd get from it.

As part of my release, I was required to enroll in the long-term outpatient Odyssey Program. For a year, we gathered in a room in the basement of the jail, sharing our stories and learning coping and anger management skills. Once a month, our group of rough-looking ex-convicts would walk through Valleyfair to ride the roller coasters or roam the trails at the Minnesota Zoo. Surrounded by kids and families, we looked like everybody else. We dined at Denny's, gathered at the movie theater, and went bowling. We'd laugh and tease each other as we took turns rolling a bowling ball through our legs, sometimes backward. Many of the guys had never been to a movie or hung out and gone to a park. I could tell some were trying to hide how good they were feeling because they weren't used to expressing it. Me included. We were caught up in our own little worlds, confined by all our secrets about how we'd lived that we didn't want anyone to know. Just being able to loosen up and be ourselves—and find ourselves—felt like letting out a deep breath.

Later, I helped start a men's recovery group with campouts and fishing trips, a place for anyone who felt like he didn't fit in anywhere. Guaranteed, you'd fit right into our men's group. If they were hesitant after being on the outside for so long, I would say, "Whatcha got to lose?" They'd hop in the van, sleep in oversized tents, chew on burgers and hot dogs, and start to feel human again. Indian Mike would call these gatherings "The Great Love."

The more I connected with others, the less I felt the need to hide or fight against being myself. When Sonny, a one-legged preacher, joined our meetings, I openly asked, "So, what happened to you?" It turned out a drunk driver had slammed into him, pinning his lower half against a wall. As a man of the church, he had listened to people's confessions, heard stories of hurt and pain, and stood beside the beds of the dying. It had left him numb inside. Then he saw our group of ten misfits, trying to keep each other sober by being real about what we'd lost. And the next moment, we'd burst into laughter after hearing someone share how he managed to have a great weekend: "Guys, I kept my mouth shut, and my wife was happy. It worked!" We lifted each other up, and Sonny was moved by all the brotherly love in that room.

When he asked if I'd drive him to northern Minnesota to see the mouth of the Mississippi—he'd grown up in Louisiana where the river ends—I said yes. We found a spot by the water, chewed on coffee grains, and marveled at the steam coming off the water. Snow-covered trees surrounded us. Then, not ten feet from us, an eagle swooped down. I had brought a camera along and snapped a few shots. When we got back, I created a small scrapbook, adding handwritten notes beside the prints about our adventure. On the cover, I wrote "Sunday with Sonny." As he flipped through the pages, tears streamed down his face. Here was another moment in my life, like reading to the kids, where something I did meant so much to someone. And I was just being myself.

That's what saved me every time I found myself searching my name on the internet, wallowing in past mistakes. I'd slump further into my chair, scrolling through my records, and think, *I'm a fucking loser, right here in black and white.* I'd spiral and imagine trying to buy a nice car one day, knowing what bankers would discover in my background checks. On the streets, I'd heard once, "You ain't never gonna be nothing than a crackhead." It pierced through me like a knife because I knew they were right. But here was this preacher letting me know I could do good, that I could *be* good, that I had something to offer another human being.

Soon after Sonny, I met Mary, a little old lady who asked to have lunch with me after an AA meeting. I thought it was weird. But even today, when I'm trying to fight myself and to walk on by, I can't. *Don't think. Don't pause. Just do it.* And when I do, sincerely and without expectation, something really fucking great happens. Our lunch became weekly. In one conversation, she shared a memory of a gold Zippo lighter that her dad had gifted her. I tracked down a similar one for her birthday a few months later. We both cried. I'd been a dirty crackhead who would have taken her purse, her twenty dollars, and ran without looking back. But I was beginning to have faith in myself as a man again. I was proud of these relationships, and if I were to use again, I knew I'd be breaking them all and letting them down.

Nowadays, when guys coming off the streets list their worst problems, I say, "Poor you? No. First off, you've got your head down. Pull back your hood, lift your head up, and be *a part of.* There are experiences and opportunities all around you. You're sitting in so much shit that your mind's cloudy and they're just passing you by. Look! Missed another one."

***

In 2012, two former sponsees who are now my best friends, Steve and Eric, separately asked me to be godfather to their babies. I broke down and wept.

Steve named his daughter Makana after a mountain range in Hawaii. Makana means "a gift, to receive." Here were Steve and his wife, both sober now, rebuilding their lives and having a baby together. We knew this child was a gift to us all. I'm her Ro-Ro, and whenever she catches a glimpse of me, she runs across the room and captures me in a bear hug.

She's almost a middle schooler now, but we're just as close. She's interested in interior design, so I gave her a budget to reimagine her room this summer. She's been thinking about paint colors, maybe an accent wall, fixtures, and a new bed. I told her she can have one month of Ro-Ro's time and I'll make her dreams come true.

My friend Eric chose his sister to be Landon's godmother and me to be his godfather. Eric considers me a brother. I met him when he'd already gotten sober and needed someone to hold him accountable. He'd never gone to college but always wanted to. When he drove to the community college to enroll, he didn't even make it out of his car. He called in a panic, and I said, "Breathe. What's this all about?" Pulling into that parking lot, full of teachers and students he didn't know, triggered memories of being forced into nine different classrooms as a child who was moved around a lot. He had numbed himself with huffing Wite-Out, then smoking weed, and eventually found meth. Now, he had me. The start of every semester was a nightmare. With every new class and every new syllabus, he'd call again, panicking, "Oh, my God,

I'm going to fail. I should just withdraw. Oh, my God!" That went on all the way through his master's in social work.

It's still hard for him, like most of us, to cope with the lingering self-doubt that he has anything good to offer. Despite everything he's accomplished, those successes just don't register as loud. There's always an excuse for why those good things happened, rather than owning he was deserving of good things and how maybe he had earned them.

As I stood in the church and signed my name to be a godparent to Landon, I steadied my hand and quieted my own doubting voice inside: "Are you sure you've got the right person?" After all these years, like Eric, the life I led was still lurking in the corners of my mind, all the people I'd let down: *You ain't never gonna be nothing than a crackhead.* I didn't have that hug from my mama or daddy. I'd been alone, trying to make my way through life, trying to navigate it, and I sucked. I'd proven that every time I reached for a crack pipe, or worse, witnessed a stranger pulling their loved one close when they caught a glimpse of me. I was less than.

These people came into my life almost like mile markers of hope. The kids at the Ronald McDonald House, Sunday with Sonny, Mondays with Mary, Eric and Steve and walking arm in arm. Each moment lifted me a little more, and a little more, till I stood erect with the trust and faith they had in me. These were the greatest moments in my life, and each one saved me. With my head down, they would have passed me by.

For the rest of my life, I have to be careful about what I do, where I go, and who I'm around. People say when you're using to just put your family first instead. But when you're using, your drug becomes the most important thing, what you care most about. Nothing else matters except where and when you'll get your next hit. I would know; I've put more dedication and love into this drug than anything else in my life. I could easily get knocked off course. Yes, I'd lose my daughter, my wife—Lilly—and my godchildren too. But this may be even more important: I'd lose sight of what's possible in life, what's possible for me, and be hunched over again. Maybe permanently this time. I never want to forget that it's a big fucking world out there with so much opportunity, and that I deserve to be in it.

So, with my shoulders pulled back, I tell people, "Look up so the sunlight can shine on your face. If you're looking down, the sun's gonna hit the back of your neck…lost on you."

Rory with his godchildren, Landon (left) and Makana (right)

Rory with his best friends Eric (top) and Steve (bottom)

TRUST WE'RE ALL DOING THE BEST WE CAN WITH WHAT WE GOT AND WHAT WE KNOW

In 2008, when Sabina was eleven years old, she and Alma approached me about Sabina maybe coming to live with me and getting to know me now. Over the years when I wasn't so high that I'd forget, I'd drive to Hastings on weekends to see Sabina. Or sometimes Alma and her husband would drop her off in Rochester. I became a "weekend dad" as my own dad had been.

We'd swing side by side at the park, or go shopping for a new pair of jeans, or make paper crafts together with whoever I was dating at the time. Or we might do all three and I'd be Super Dad. Sabina would bounce down the stairs and excitedly say, "Daddy's great!" My heart would skip a beat every time Sabina looked at me like I was the coolest person in the world. It was an easy gig, but I knew it wasn't true parenting. I didn't have to deal with the tired little girl at the end of the day like Alma and her husband did.

I looked at Sabina; she was older now. Her straight black hair looked just like her mom's, and she wore glasses. She could be so quiet at first, then get so chatty once she trusted you. She chewed on her sleeve, something she did when she was nervous. How many mornings had already passed when I wasn't around to say, "Good morning," to her? How many afternoons had I missed hearing all of the happy chatter of what happened at school that day? I leaned over and whispered, "You can come home with me."

When the move-in day came, with Sabina sitting next to me on the drive to Rochester, reality sank in. Robbery. Assaults. Drugs. Disorderly conduct. Jail time in multiple counties. How the fuck did I think it was a good idea for a crack addict from the streets of Minneapolis to raise a little girl? What did I do?

The next morning, as I lounged across the couch, Sabina woke up and moaned, "Daddy, I'm hungry." Aw, shit. Everyday, "What's for dinner?... I'm tired... I want to be in the school play... Can I join the band and play the flute?" I was busting my ass just trying to put food on the table. How the hell was I going to get a flute? But I did. I searched Craigslist postings and picked up a used one from a lady in Elgin. Four nights a week, I parked my car at Willow Creek Middle School and read from my AA book while she had band or play practice. Every single year, she was in a fucking play.

***

After work one night, I heard whimpering from behind her closed bedroom door. Sabina was getting older, and some boy must have pissed her off. Aw, shit. Been working all day, what was I supposed to do? I knocked on her door. "Bina?" More whimpering. When I tiptoed in, she turned her face toward me, tears pouring. Robotically, I asked, "So, what's going on? A boy?" She nodded. Well, I couldn't snap his knuckles, some twelve-year-old thug of a kid. I miserably thought I'd have to hug her now; the idea scared me as I had no practice. I slumped beside her and awkwardly threw a stiff arm around her shoulders. "Oh, it'll be okay." My hand patted her like a dying fish, desperate to be put out of its misery.

After years on the street, I didn't know how to comfort a preteen or give hope and care. I'd been trained to be cautious. On Lake Street, in Minneapolis, everybody was out to get something from you. They'd pretend to be your friend, and you'd get high and pass out, only to realize later that your shoes were gone, your money was gone, or your pipe, your lighter, your three cigarettes you were glad you still had left, all gone. That time in my life made a lasting impression. They'd ask for one cigarette and grab your whole pack when you took it out. I stiffened any time I heard a fast and loose, "Hey, buddy…" because I knew they were no real friend. I learned to keep my emotions close, and I recognize now this showed up as a kind of neglect for my daughter.

I was never that someone she could eat a bucket of ice cream with or sit beside and cry on. As Indian Mike would say, I'd felt sorry for myself for so long I'd used up all my sympathy on myself. I failed miserably at creating that kind of bond with Sabina. I knew she needed her mama. When I learned Alma was battling her own addiction to prescription medication, sometimes we'd all meet up at the mall so the two of them could talk. She did her best to be a good mom. She was there when Sabina was a child and I wasn't. For all those early years of basketball practices, Girl Scouts meetings, and playdates. For the longest time, it was Alma's husband who woke up on Saturday mornings to watch reruns of cartoons with Sabina. Now, it was my turn to step up.

I know I wasn't the Super Dad that Sabina had been used to on the weekends-only gig, but I did what I had to so I could provide for her basic needs. It might have been a frozen dinner, but we always had a roof over our heads. Always. When we were denied medical assistance, I made such a scene at the government center that two sheriffs had to escort me out. I lost it. "I'm a single dad! I can barely pay rent. I'm making fifteen dollars an hour working my ass off at Rob's Construction, living in a house the size of a shed, and working six fucking days a week. I need to keep a day to heal! Don't you guys understand? I don't even want insurance. I'm just telling you to insure *her*!"

My application was denied. They said I made too much, but they didn't look at all the bills I had to pay, that hardly anything was left over. I was still paying off my criminal fines from over the years and my culinary school loan too. (When I finally paid off my debt, I half expected a Publishers Clearing House moment, complete with balloons and applause. Or at least a letter congratulating me. In the end, I owed money and paid it back. That was that.)

I felt defeated, but I knew my daughter needed health insurance. I researched online, filled out complicated forms, talked to the people I needed to, and figured out how to get her insured. To pay for it, I started working Sundays too. I worked late, and when I wasn't at Rob's Construction, I attended AA meetings. Some days, I'd see Sabina at eight at night and then it was time for bed. She was alone a lot and had to grow up fast. She kept the house clean, washed the dishes, shopped for groceries, and lined our freezer with stacks of ready-to-eat dinners. When she was old enough, she got a job and earned her own shopping money.

One night, Sabina begged me to bring her to an informational session about an upcoming New York-DC school trip. It was the first time I had ever seen her sit still for twenty whole minutes, no wiggling, no noise, no being distracted by some boy, just completely captivated. I watched parents pull out their checkbooks, while I checked my eighty-dollar account balance online. Watching her excitement during the presentation, I knew my little girl was going on that trip. She needed this. We sold Butter Braid pastries all over town to raise money. We hit up places like AA, Walmart, Kwik Trip, and Cub Foods and worked and laughed together along the way.

We snuck in more of our version of quality family time when she came to holiday events at the Pioneer Club on days when kids were welcome. There was the Fourth of July celebration, the New Year's Eve party, and cookouts at parks across Rochester. After a while, Sabina started attending meetings too. She listened as people shared their stories, and even though she heard things beyond her age, she understood the reality of life and how badly and quickly things could slip. She adjusted to life as the daughter of an AA member, but I knew she still longed for a more normal life, like playing board games by the fireplace after a home-cooked meal.

I feared relapsing and needed to stay close to that community. I had things to do now and places to be. I couldn't smoke crack because there were men relying on me to show up or call. I cared about them and wanted to make sure they were doing okay. I didn't hate the holidays anymore. I was busy—I had fruit trays to deliver, three sponsees were inviting me over for turkey, and I was in the middle of securing a campsite for the upcoming men's group outing. The stuff I used to stew about and knock down a Bacardi Coke to forget I didn't have time for anymore. Because of AA I crowded my schedule out of fear that if I gave myself even an inch, I'd lose everything. People would approach Sabina after meetings, expecting the same wild energy I carried, but she was a quiet reflector. While I focused on my intentionally long to-do list, my daughter sat there by herself.

As she got older, Sabina worked her way up to larger roles in the school play. I watched her in *Oliver Twist* from the back row—she was the cruel matron of the orphanage—and I thought, "Damn, she's good! All those years of being annoyed by having to drive her to rehearsals, and she was up there rocking it." It was the same with band. Back in middle school, it was just noise. I'd heard Beethoven before and that wasn't it. But when she started at Mayo High School, she was second or third chair, playing soulful solos on her flute. The emotion in the music would wash over me, and I'd get goosebumps and tear up. That was my kid up there. I'd done something right.

***

Growing up with Alma, from preschool to third grade, Sabina had bounced across multiple schools—from Hastings to Red Wing back to Hastings to Eden Prairie to Shakopee to Belle Plaine. Friendships felt superficial, torn between these moves; she never had enough time to form deep connections. Now, in high school, she admitted she befriended whoever would have her, and they weren't always nice. At parties, she'd chug whatever they dared her to in exchange for the smallest crumb of their friendship or approval. (I found out later that she gave her final AP Human Geography presentation while still drunk from the night before.) At lunchtime, they'd joke with hostility, "Everyone, put your money away. Here comes the Jew girl!"

Food had always been a source of comfort to her, but as she grew into her teenage years, her insecurity about her body image grew too. I questioned her about what she ate and how much. When she needed emotional nurturing, I tried to fix the problem by counting calories and missed the reasons behind it. The bullying worsened as her "friends" grabbed at her body and used crude nicknames.

When the Sweetheart Dance was coming up, she finally had something to look forward to. She even went dress shopping with a friend and her mom all the way to the Mall of America. But at school the next morning, her boyfriend changed his status to "single" and stonewalled her. Then she was handed a report card she wasn't expecting. All in the same period. To someone with consistently straight As, with maybe a B here and there, seeing her first C was the real tragedy. She lost the one thing she could always count on for praise: that she was like her dad and always did so well in school. That must have been the final straw.

Our worlds collided and crashed when Sabina tried to kill herself during her freshman year. She swallowed a bunch of pills and sat under a downtown bridge while melting snow poured down all around her. She called my girlfriend for help before she lost consciousness. They rushed her to Generose, the Mayo Clinic's psychiatric facility. I sat beside her hospital bed and cried over her. During "no visitor hours," I climbed the hill behind the building and planted a sign large enough for her to see from her window. It said, "I love you, Bina Bina."

Sabina doesn't know this, but without a single doubt in my mind, if she didn't exist, I wouldn't be here today. When she was little, she'd clamp onto my leg and I'd pretend to be a monster, walking around with a thirty-pound weight strapped to me. She'd giggle, getting louder and louder. How that sound fills you up… it's priceless. Smiling up at me whenever I walked through the door. No drug can give you that. That unconditional love is why I'm alive today, and why I've continued to fight, through this cancer too.

During group sessions at Generose, Sabina said the other kids would spend their time complaining about how they didn't belong there. But not her. "I almost died, Dad. I know this is where I'm supposed to be right now." She was in a place where she could be honest with herself about where her pain was coming from without judgment. But those ten days of learning about coping skills and positive self-talk were no match for the years of high school drama still ahead.

When she dumped Inta Juice over someone's head at lunch, we were both called to the assistant principal's office for her inappropriate behavior. I stormed in there. "Why do you think she did it? Did you ever consider that he didn't like what she was wearing and was calling her names?" Ultimately, they spoke to the young man too (he had tried to take pictures of her without her consent), but the damage was done.

With Sabina hurting so much, I told Alma that our daughter was about to turn eighteen and leave for college soon. If she wanted to rebuild a relationship with her daughter, now was the time. Alma picked her up. I was supportive because I believe every little girl needs her mama. Sabina completed her senior year online and earned her high school diploma. She went to college in South Carolina, and toward the end of her freshman year, she called me from her dorm room. "Dad! Dad! I won a speech contest! And you wanna know the best part? I don't have to do any more work in the class and get an automatic A!"

I matched her enthusiasm. "Sabina, that's awesome! What'd you write about?"

She answered with one word: "You."

Dear Dad,

As my first year of college comes to a close, I find myself living by that AA Big Book quote you always say: "One day at a time." It keeps me sane some days. However, in times of quiet, my mind wanders and I can't help but reflect on the years we spent living together. You're an accomplished man. You're also the first to admit that you were quite the opposite when it came to parenting. We used to joke that as long as I was still breathing, there was milk in the fridge, and cereal in the cupboard, that was good enough. I resented you though. I saw our science experiment, a single father raising his adolescent daughter, as an utter failure. Maybe it was time, or maturity, or seeing that gray hairs had taken over your already balding head when you came to visit that changed my mind, but I think I was wrong. I'm sure you're grinning at that. Overall, I'm beginning to think that maybe—just maybe—our experiment was a success.

It was hopeless at the time. I grew up too fast. As a teenager in suburbia, it felt strange to be working forty hours a week and trudging through the snow with my arms full of groceries. Meanwhile, my friends were delivering newspapers and coming home to meatloaf. I had the house to myself so often. It felt like having my own apartment. Everyone was jealous, but I was lonely. I dealt with that by getting into trouble. You know it's bad when you're sixteen and your dad doesn't notice that you haven't come home until the second night. Whether it was partying or sour relationships, I found myself asking the same question: Where were my parents? It didn't help that I had struggled with mental illness since third grade. You really had no idea what to do with that. I remember one day we were sitting in your truck and you said to me that if I was just going to lie to my therapist about how bad things were, you were going to stop funding it.

My mother was unpredictable to say the least. It was clear that you hated her for it. At times, it felt as though you thought you were better than her because you sobered up first and I never had to see firsthand all the terrible things that you did. Things were almost always hostile between the two of you. The last time I remember you getting along was when I was in middle school. I remember the night clearly in my mind. We went to a meeting where she received a one-day sobriety keychain. She gave it to me when I left for college, and I keep it with me always so I'll never forget that night.

You tried though. You were always trying. You have this love of life that you want to share with everyone. Eventually, this passion rubbed off on me and we did some pretty incredible things together. My twelfth birthday for instance. There were over a hundred people, a giant tent in our front yard, and a DJ who even had a fog machine. It rained the whole day, but I think it made it that much better. We went to concerts together, and in the eighth grade, you gave me the opportunity to go to Washington, DC, and New York City. Although the trip was fun, I think fundraising for it might have been better. We sold Butter Braid out of the bed of your truck at AA meetings. And there was that night I had to speak at your five-year anniversary. I finally realized why you were so passionate about sharing your story with others, even if it can be scary to speak in front of a crowd.

As great as these things were, it is often the less remarkable things that mean the most. Many nights were spent at the dining table just talking about life, not even realizing how late it was getting. Together, we learned valuable lessons from your quest to improve your credit score and the challenge of using less electricity than our neighbors. My favorite was when I was in a production of The Music Man. *All of your friends came and you spent the whole time in the back making a ruckus. Even with your busy schedule, you came to every band concert, somehow surviving the awkward squawks of middle school.*

We had an interesting little life for ourselves. In the words of Charles Dickens in A Tale of Two Cities, *"It was the best of times, it was the worst of times, it was the age of wisdom, it was the age of foolishness, it was the epoch of belief." I spent too much time ridiculing you that some of my best memories were lost. But now I see all of the things that I learned from you. I look at my peers, and for better or worse, I see their parents in them. When I turn and look at myself, I see so much of you. I'm finally content with that. Nowadays, when you tell me that you're proud of me, I believe you. That makes me so happy. What brings me the most joy, however, is that I can look you in the eye and tell you that I'm proud of you too.*[2]

Another moment that saved me.

***

Sabina transferred to a university in upstate New York to study public policy. She had big dreams of going to law school, surrounded herself with a supportive group of friends, and even had plans to apply for an internship at the New York State Senate. She was doing everything right, but her world came crashing down when she lost her eligibility for student loans. Grandma Sabina, her namesake, was her cosigner, but she had to step back when she helped Alma purchase a house. The rest of us were rejected as cosigners. When Sabina had to leave school and move back home with Grandma, I knew she was going through a tough time, but it wasn't till later that I learned she had spiraled into a cycle of daily drinking and popping Adderall. We were talking less and less, and a distance grew between us. That's when Grandma died.

---

[2] Reprinted with permission.

Grandma Sabina, originally from the Philippines, had escaped an abusive relationship before she could even speak English. She walked barefoot across central Minnesota till she found someone willing to help her with a fresh start. She taught herself English while working in a factory in Hastings. Her small stature contained so much quiet strength.

Since the moment I met her, Grandma Sabina never held anything against me, even through my addiction. She was the kind of person who would love you, no matter what you were going through in life. It was always, "Hey, Rory, how's it going? Did you eat today? Let me feed you." There was always a pot of something bubbling on the stove, and she'd laugh at all my inappropriate jokes. Even with my stints in jail and my hands in weed, coke, meth, and crack, she never judged me. She and Alma's stepdad wanted me to do well because I was Sabina's father; they wanted me to be there for her.

Grandma Sabina was my daughter's rock, the only constant in her life from the time she was born. The person Sabina could count on to answer or call back within five minutes.

Sabina was at home when her grandma asked to lie down. She often had dizzy spells over the past few years, but now she moaned, "This is the worst I've ever felt." To distract her from the pain, Sabina talked about an afternoon when they went to Dairy Queen for ice cream. She remembered how Grandma Sabina would always get a banana split. That was their last conversation before a brain aneurysm ruptured.

Twenty-five years earlier, I stood in my dad's living room watching the most stabilizing person in my life die. Now, Sabina was doing the same. I couldn't protect her from that. At the hospital, Alma, Sabina, and her uncles held Grandma's hand and then unplugged her.

After two years of near silence, Sabina called me. "I miss you, Dad. I've been a coward and haven't talked about how bad things have been. I'd love it if you visited me. I'd like to catch up." I invited her to move back to Rochester, closer to me. She packed her things and eventually confided that she'd been living on her own for a while. She could now tell me what it was like to go hungry and to freeze in Minnesota winters. She'd found a sense of gratitude for how we had survived when she was young.

She started therapy again and shared one night, "You know, Dad, for the longest time, I thought that one day, I'd wake up and everything would be perfect. I thought that if I could just get out of here, if I could just find a job, or if I could just go back to school, if I could just get my degree, that everything would magically fall into place and I'd be healed. Well, I don't know if any of that will ever happen, but I can still be okay. I'm ready to stop grading myself now and fighting how I think my life should have gone. It went the only way it could have. You were doing the best you could with what you had and what you knew. It's what we're all doing."

Rory with young Sabina

GOT A DREAM? GO! I'LL HOLD THE DOOR FOR YOU.

Before Sabina ever came to live with me, I sat down with Indian Mike and started in again, "You know, one day, I'm going to..." He raised his hand and stopped me. Leaning against the table for support, he rose from his seat and made his way to the door. He swung it wide open for me.

"Go ahead. What's stopping you? There's a big ol' world out there. Go get it. You have all these dreams, how you want your own house and to make more money and to meet someone... What are you doing sitting here and talking about it? Go! I'll hold the door for ya. I'm tired of listening to you. Why don't you go do something?"

I opened my mouth to argue but swallowed the words. He was right...again. In the years leading up to the 2008 housing market crash, banks were quick to grant mortgage loans. I may have had a criminal record with gaps in my credit history, but I'd been a loyal employee at Rob's Construction for over five years. I was approved for a loan on a small house on Seventh Street, a foreclosure that had been on the market for a year.

The exterior siding had three different colors: old, older, and oldest. A large piece of plywood, covered in graffiti, dangled out front where a window should have been. People would drive up for a look and U-turn right out the driveway. But me? When they handed me the keys, I stepped into the house with a rush of memories from my stays in shelters, halfway houses, and motel rooms—and I cried. I fucking *owned* this house. It may have been missing a working bathroom, but it was beautiful to me. (And I made every single payment on time, too.)

When my buddies asked, "What the hell are you gonna do with this place?" I answered with a smile, "You'll see." It took a couple of years, one project and permit at a time, to make them see what I always knew the place could be. At one point, I had the entire roof torn off when a neighbor walked over and yelled up at me, "Sir! Sir! Those clouds are coming in fast!" I sped to Menards, grabbed a massive tarp, and quickly pulled it over the gaping hole. In the end, I had a newly added second-level floor with a vaulted ceiling, a kitchen lined with maple wood cabinets, a master bedroom with a private walkout deck, and fresh siding and flooring throughout. Kenny, who was still my boss at Rob's, suggested getting roommates, but I had a different plan in mind.

I always believed there was a missing piece in our system. When guys would get out of treatment and structured living, that's when they'd often fail. They needed a place to go, something more relaxed than a halfway house, where they could be surrounded by others who were staying sober every day. My house on Seventh Street became a sort of recovery home with three or four roommates to come home to, and people to talk to at the end of the day and go to a meeting with.

It beat sitting alone in an apartment under a single lightbulb, trapped in your own thoughts. That's dangerous for a man trying to stay sober. You start thinking, what's one hit or drink going to hurt; I deserve it. You sell yourself on it. Damn, we can be the best salesmen we've ever met, our own worst enemy. That's why I'd hang out at the Pioneer Club, sometimes going an hour early or on nights without meetings. I didn't want to sit by myself with a paycheck in my hand on a Friday night. Instead, I smoked cigarettes, drank coffee, and felt safe.

***

When I shared with Indian Mike that I'd met a girl in AA and we were going on a date, he said, straight-faced, "Rory, you ride a fucking bike. What are you going to do? Have her stand on foot pegs while you ride to Denny's? You have nothing to offer a rat right now. What are you doing? How do you think that's going to end? You really think that's a good idea?"

I needed his straight talk. What would have happened was that she and I would have gotten high together and made each other sick. So many people start to do well and then jump into a relationship or run into old friends they partied with before. Recovery is no longer their priority and they crash hard. That was the first of many times his no-bullshit truth saved me. I listened and waited.

At that point, my relationships with women had been hot-cold, up-down, always unpredictable. I'd react by ripping right out of the driveway. I remembered Diane, the waitress at the Levee Cafe I dated back in Hastings. We'd fight and she'd smash dishes. She even threw a phone hanging from a corded handset across the room once and it hit my face. People at work would joke, "Look at that fat lip, or should we call it AT&T long distance?" We'd laugh, but I knew I was in a terrible relationship. We took turns getting domestic assault charges handed to us. It was a matter of whose story the cops believed when they showed up. When she got her second charge, I put new locks on the door and called her mom. "Come get her things. I'm done." I still have that scar on my lip.

Now, I was this scorned, hurt, scared, emotional, afraid to commit, broken, scarred thing from the street. Like a cornered raccoon snarling inside a trash can. In 2006, a year into my sobriety, I met Viola, who was just like me. With the road I've been on, I can see all the years of shit people have trudged through in their eyes. Viola had three children with three different exes, and none of them had been very nice to her.

We made a little life together. She took care of the home, cooked meals, and looked after her kids. I helped where I could by driving everyone where they needed to go. To help her progress, I moved into her apartment and rented out my Seventh Street house to men in recovery. Now, I was able to help pay a share of the rent. I purposely didn't rush in to just save her; I wanted her to own that she was the one making her life improvements happen—from getting a car, to having her own place, to getting her kids back.

I still have this outlook. Even as I've grown financially secure, I fight the urge to swoop in and take care of everything for Sabina. The truth is, I don't know how much time I have left, and I want her to learn how to land on her two feet. Over the past year, she's been paying her own rent, and I couldn't be more proud of her. If I were to just give all the time, it wouldn't teach that lesson. No, I won't stand by and silently watch the people I love suffer (after

all, I'm a dad), but from my days of begging on street corners, I
know the value of a dollar and want them to understand too. Life
is unpredictable and things can get tough real quick. If you're used
to getting everything you want, you have no fucking defense. I
don't want my daughter like that. Or my godchildren when they're
older, either. Me? I can live in a shed in the woods and start over
again. I want them to know that if their world ever flips upside
down, they'll be able to rise from the dirt and fucking fight for
what they need, want, and believe in too.

I was with Viola for years, and from living with a woman with
three kids, I learned how to be a partner in a relationship, to be a
fucking man and be responsible. Her two youngest just loved me,
and I'd take them places, sometimes with Sabina who was ten then
and still living with Alma. Once, we rented a suite at Kalahari
Resorts and would run laughing from one water ride to the next.
But her oldest, Jordan, resented my presence. She'd give me the
"who the fuck are you" death stare. For most of her life, she'd
watched how men treated her mom and siblings and was
disappointed over and over again. She'd taken on the role of
protector, and now here was another man making grand gestures.

It took two full years before we turned a corner. We stood by
a river, and I cried from my heart. "You don't have to like me, but
I'm here at your mom's side, and I love your brother and sister.
You can hate me, but I'm going to keep loving you." She caught
me in a hug, and we both cried. I often sponsored people coming
off the streets, but man, with Jordan, I learned the real meaning
of a hard case.

Viola and I experienced so many firsts in our time together,
with that bubbly joy of kids. We held stable jobs, I became a
proud homeowner, and we created holiday traditions. On Easter,

we'd go overboard on candy and baskets for the kids. Once, we caught her son with a smear of chocolate on the back of his neck. How the heck did he manage that?

But Viola's first time in a dress was something special. On one of our first dates, I'd tried to surprise her with a kiss but she instinctively cowered with her hands over her face. I'd thought, what the fuck. Are you okay? She'd had her jaw broken by a man. Little by little, I gained her trust, and then planned a whole evening experience for her. I picked her up and watched as she nervously tugged at her dress and wobbled in heels. It took my breath away. All night long, I handed her sticky notes with messages like, "Hey, if I had one wish, I'd be here with you." Cheesy lines, but there was real feeling behind them. When we got to the top floor of the Kahler Grand Hotel, a saxophone player I'd hired was playing Kenny G. I handed her the last note: "Will you dance with me?" My shoulder was damp from her tears, and we moved to the music under the sparkling downtown lights.

I learned to listen long enough to understand what Viola loved and dreamed of. She collected little glass and ceramic dolphins at truck stops. When I asked if she'd ever seen one in real life, she told me she'd never even been on a plane before. I saved up at Rob's Construction and took her down to Sea World. We watched the show with the dancing dolphins, and afterward, she got to touch and feed them by hand. When I looked over, she was trembling and choking back tears. For a woman who had struggled with a meth addiction and trusting men, to be so innocent now, full of joy and experiencing a dream, that meant everything to me.

She'd sometimes say, "I'll fucking cut a bitch if she keeps looking at ya." We'd laugh, but she grew to be protective of me, and it felt nice to be wanted. We had plans to get married. She got a dress, and we put a deposit down on a venue and even picked out a cake. But when the day came closer, I felt the full weight of maintaining a full-time job at Rob's, the back-and-forth of taking kids here and there, juggling custody arrangements, and trying to be a good dad to four kids. And that meant making time for all of their different school activities. All while maintaining my sobriety. When I pictured our future, it was crowded and busy. In the end, I backed out of the wedding.

Over our years together, we'd argue about her baby daddies and their involvement in our lives, split up for a while, and then get back together. Once, I'd come home to her ex sitting at my kitchen counter eating my leftover chicken, the same meal I'd been daydreaming about all day at work. The same guy who didn't contribute a dime to the household. I'd lost it. But this time, when Viola left, she found another guy. Someone kind and handsome. She'd chosen someone, and it wasn't me. We were done. I went to Treasure Island as a distraction, where my friend, Dale, met me, and I cried.

Over the next months, I put on a pair of sweatpants and went for runs around Silver Lake before getting a membership at the Rochester Athletic Club. I made it a point to lift weights and run on the treadmill every day, and I channeled the loss into getting healthy. I'd been a two-pack-a-day chain-smoker since I was fourteen, when I smoked my first cigarette with David in the woods that we'd stolen from Mom. Determined to quit, I stuck Nicorette patches on my arm. They required a prescription, but a girl from AA hooked me up. When I was almost out of patches, I cut one into halves and the last one into thirds just to make them last.

Even though our breakup was tough, Viola and I will always

share a deep connection through the countless firsts we experienced together. It's why we're still friends today. During Sabina's hospitalization after her suicide attempt, Viola wrote her a card of encouragement and support, which Sabina still keeps close. And I'm Viola's rock, someone she can rely on to build her up in moments of self-doubt. Her children even wrote me heartbreaking letters when they first learned I was sick with cancer. Her oldest, Jordan, too: *I was always hard on you and never even gave you a chance. I'm sorry, and if you ever need anything, I'll be there.* The same goes for me.

***

In 2013, a year after breaking things off with Viola for the last time, a few guys from AA waved me over after a meeting. "Want to come to church with us today?" Their church had a band, and we rocked out to the music up front. I'm a Jewish guy who's all about this type of joy; it spoke to me, and I joined right in. For a string of Sundays, we met up for breakfast at the Caribou on Second Street and then drove over to the Community Celebration Church in the next town.

Out in the crowd, a cute blond girl giggled and smiled as she watched us try to dance. When I caught her eyes, she turned away. I tried to be as cool as I could, but I must have been trying too hard because she really did stop looking. Week after week, I'd see her, and when I finally built up the courage to speak to her, I couldn't hold her attention. Later, she confessed she was distracted by the bedazzled bling on the back pockets of my jeans and couldn't get past it.

I kept suggesting places for us to meet up, and one day she

surprised both of us when she answered, "Well, why not? What the hell? Let's do it." Lilly, who was twenty-three, wasn't attracted to me and had no interest in pursuing a relationship with anyone. She was new to Rochester and just out of treatment at the Pathway House. She didn't have a single friend in town and was bored in her little apartment between her shifts at Quiznos. She had nothing to lose by saying yes.

Meanwhile, I was forty-two with a mouthful of braces, complete with pink bands. When I pulled up on my blue chopper and revved the engine, I saw her take a few horrified steps back. I was wearing a tight black shirt with large printed angel wings. She climbed on behind me, hesitant, and when I told her to hold on, she barely gripped my waist with the tips of her index fingers. This chick had never been on a bike before. I took it slow, but she hated every second. We got to the restaurant and I pounded down a plate of nachos. When I smiled at her, it was with bits of chips and cheese stuck to my braces. With another bite, I added hot wings to the mix.

For the rest of the evening, I literally sat on my hands, repeating to myself, "Don't touch her. Don't you dare. You're dirty." Inside, I was walking on ice, extending a foot out to lightly tap it, to test its strength, cautiously at first because you think it'll break. When you know it's strong enough, you take another step. And then another. Yes, Lilly had battled alcohol addiction, but with loving parents and a stable home life where family would gather for the holidays, she was still clear-eyed, glowing, and pure. She was like a delicate butterfly gently landing for a moment on a little flower; I was scared to get too close. In those early days, before every date, I'd force myself to look in the mirror and tell myself, "Well, why not me? Why can't I be with someone like her?"

One date became two, then five, then ten. I took Lilly to Lake

City and rented a catamaran sailboat. She'd grown up riding in her parents' boat and I knew she would love it. We closed our eyes to the breeze and eventually docked at one of the islands for a picnic dinner I'd prepared just for her. As the sun set, we ate grilled shrimp and fresh fruit, with Taylor Swift, her favorite singer, playing in the background.

Lilly told me she'd never known anyone to give her this kind of attention, someone who was careful and patient with her. How could I not be? I saw how gentle she was with my godchildren, how she would kneel down to their level and genuinely connect with them. Or when she saw a picture of a lost dog and her first instinct was to help.

When I introduced her to Sabina, she immediately noticed how much Lilly looked like Grandma Arnell, my mother. The same square face, medium-length blonde hair, with kind, welcoming eyes that twinkled with warmth. And Lilly's soft-spokenness only helped to highlight the moments when she would hold me accountable for speaking or acting too rashly. Sabina liked Lilly—someone who could make her dad think twice. They bonded over their love of history and classic literature. And the fact that Lilly was always ready to say yes to experiences and adventures, just like me, was a bonus. She wasn't into fishing, but would still agree to come along as company. I'd fish while she'd read and stop to take pictures when I caught something.

During our first Hanukkah together, on the eighth night, I surprised Lilly with a gift—a two-week trip to Puerto Rico, just the two of us. I was working all the time at Rob's and juggling what activities I could of Sabina's. Life was hectic, so I intentionally made space and time for Lilly. Her days were busier too when she added a second job and was walking everywhere. I told her she could use my car any time she needed. My grand gestures expressed what I felt but knew she wasn't ready to hear.

During one of our dates, she confessed, "I don't understand why you're even interested in me when you have your shit together and I clearly don't in my studio apartment. Is this just pity?" I was in love with a woman who thought I was too good to be true. Me, who'd eaten dinner out of trash cans. Whenever I caught a glimpse of her from a distance, without her noticing, I was certain this was the girl I wanted to spend the rest of my life with. Whatever challenges came our way, we'd figure it out together.

A few months into our relationship, we rode in the Ronald McDonald Charity Bike Ride together. As we raced down winding roads into Rushford, I could feel Lilly's hands tightly wrapped around me on my blue chopper. I sensed it before she later expressed that evening, "If I can trust you with my life, I can trust you with my heart."

Every Saturday, we attended an AA meeting together. On one particular morning, I stopped the car beneath a bridge near Century High School, pretending there was something wrong with a tire. She didn't suspect a thing. Then, I handed Lilly a cup of coffee and asked her, "Do you see it?" Above us, inside the fencing, I'd arranged red Solo cups, spelling out, "I LOVE LILLY R." When she shook her head with embarrassment, I said, "I told you I'd make myself look like a fool for you."

I don't know how, but she fell in love with me—like a shooting star you hear about, but never expect to see. I had to ask, "Why me?"

Lilly finally set me straight. "Why not you, Rory? You have this incredible way of embracing people for who they are, wherever they may be in their lives. It's so freeing. I'm often thinking, 'How would Rory approach this?' You understand others' perspectives better than most of us. It's your open mind and heart… It inspires me."

We're nineteen years apart, so Lilly was nervous when she introduced me to her dad for the first time. What was he going to think of this guy? But he was happy to see her glowing after a decade of ER visits for chronic alcohol use. Her parents accepted the relationship. If this would be good for her, they were on board.

While Lilly and I were dating, we'd often have lunch at the People's Co-Op downtown, our afternoon rendezvous spot. After two years together, we discussed planning a wedding. She was adamant she didn't want the big white dress with everyone's eyes on her. Through her active addiction, she felt her family had already given her enough attention over the years. So, on December 7, 2014, we had a small ceremony right inside the café area at the People's Co-Op. Kenny and his wife were there, and Lilly's parents too.

Lilly and I had loved Puerto Rico so much that we honeymooned there for two weeks. We even hired a photographer to follow us around for a day in San Juan. I wore a white button-down shirt with a wide collar and a black suit jacket, while she had a long, flowing white dress that gracefully wrapped at her waist, with small pearl earrings. These became our wedding photos. My wife's drop-dead beautiful, someone who could model for magazine covers. And then there's me, bald, big-nosed, with a weirdly shaped head. I told the camera guy just to crop me out already.

In my darkest moment, when I had broken down on the jail cell floor, ready to end it all, a tiny flicker of hope had surfaced— a dream of having a partner one day.

Lilly and I make a pretty badass team in our lifestyle, in how we manage our home, our finances, and work. I don't compare my life to someone else's. I just look at my own situation, my own life, how it's been, and how it is now. Things aren't perfect, but there's no more emotional up-and-down craziness. When we have a problem, I don't run anymore. We talk, sometimes coming to an answer, but always listening to understand. We added two puppies to our family too—Rico (named after Puerto Rico) and Perla (after La Perla, a town near San Juan). All of this because I took a chance and let myself believe I was worthy of love.

While I continued sponsoring men in recovery, I gradually took a step back from my leadership roles at AA. I had started to feel like Forrest Gump, who runs and runs, days becoming months becoming years. And one day, he just stops. He looks up and says, "I'm pretty tired. I think I'll go home now." I was attending meetings, leading the men's group, speaking at AA events, chairing the Tradition Three AA group, and accepting speaking engagements across the state. One night, as I was sharing my story with a recovery group, I looked at my newly married wife who was sitting in the back and quietly smiling. I stopped, and like Forrest, I realized, "I'm ready to go to my wife now and give my time to her."

Whenever I took on projects, I could never do anything halfway. With the men's group, I was out organizing road trips, arranging grillouts and picnics, and extending invitations to the whole town. Even if I tried to limit myself to one day a week, the next thing I knew, they'd ask for a volunteer for something, and I'd have my hand raised. For years, I devoted every free minute to recovery efforts in this town. No one knows that better than Sabina, who'd come home to an empty house. What you put into something is what you get out of it. I was making a conscious choice now to devote more of my time to my wife, my daughter, and my work and see what I could do.

I was ready.

Rory with Lilly on his blue chopper

Rory spells out "I Love Lilly R" with red Solo cups

Rory with Lilly and their dogs, Rico and Perla

YOU *CAN.* I'LL SHOW YOU.

When I first get to know a sponsee, I'll often hear, "But you don't know me. You don't understand what I'm going through. I'll never..." They'll pick themselves apart, how they're not smart enough, how they're a felon, how they'll never get a job or get anyone to rent to them. I have a standing offer for anyone I meet: "Just come sit down with me for thirty minutes and I'll change the way you think." I'm confident that I can, that my words will play in their mind like a nagging tune they can't stop humming. When they take me up on my invitation, I start by saying, "Let's talk about your addiction."

"Well, what do you want to know? My worst? I remember..." and I'll watch their eyes drift toward painful memories. As they share their story, I'll interject sincere questions to bait them for more details. "Really?! You did? What happened after that? No way!" By the time we're done, I'll have tricked them into proving to themselves just how much drive they have. Most of us, in our addiction, have shown our determination. We just need reminders.

After Mexico, I'd wandered the streets of Rochester, even in freezing temperatures. There was a perpetual line of people in front of the Dorothy Day House, and if you wanted any chance of getting in, you had to be in line by 4 p.m. On the nights they reached capacity, I'd make my way to the laundromat off Twelfth Street. If I was lucky, I'd find a dryer that had just been run and press my back against its warmth. On crack, I didn't sleep for days. So, I'd just sit there. The laundromat had a wall of windows facing the street, and in the early morning hours, I would see police cars passing by, scanning for people like me. "You gotta keep moving," they'd warn. My backup spot was an apartment building near Mayo High School, even farther away from the laundromat. I'd force my frozen fingers to pop the lock with an old motel key card, and once inside, shuffle straight to the utility room to thaw out next to the water heater.

I've dedicated more time, money, affection, and emotional feeling to this drug than to anything or anyone else in my life. And I've proven it. For this love, I've slept in my car and in basements of filthy crackhouses. For this love, I've eaten food from the trash bin and stood starving in ten-degree weather, trying to collect quarters for one more hit. I've roamed through the streets as White Boy Fred at two in the morning, hooked on crack, where people would get shot every day. And I'm still here today? I didn't want to live that way, and yet I would have done anything, endured anything, for that high. You have to be ambitious as shit to do all that.

People struggling with alcoholism, drug addiction, and homelessness are strong people. Actions speak louder than words. That action might be to get more liquor—it's sad what we're working so hard for—but no one can deny our drive. And it's actually encouraging in a way. It means, if we want to fucking do something, we'll make it happen. Bring it on. I've had hundreds of conversations with people battling addictions where I reflect the truth of their journey and hope that a little bit of light shines through. They just need someone like me to look them in the eye and tell them they have all the ability in the world. They've already shown it. In our addiction, we've shown it. Let's incorporate it into something good now.

***

When I got married to Lilly in 2014, I'd been working at Rob's Construction for nearly fifteen years. I started with the ice dams, then became a yard bitch, moved to a roofing crew, then siding, and worked my way up to the foreman of the window crew. Now, I was Kenny's right-hand man and kept an eye on all the crews. He gave me a new truck to drive every three years on lease, and the company paid for a gas card and cell phone. But I wanted more. Not money, really; I just felt this couldn't be it for me till the end of time.

Kenny talked about how he was getting older, how he wanted to sell the company to me. All of it. I dressed up, met with attorneys, and drew up loan papers. I didn't have much money, so he was really helping me out with the reduced sale amount. But on the final day of signing, there were parts of the company he wanted to hold on to that would have severely limited my profit margins and my ability to make loan payments.

Kenny had given my daughter and me so much when we needed it, making sure we had a warm house, a working truck, and enough groceries. He'd ask, "Are you guys okay? Need any extra money for the holidays to get your daughter something?" It wasn't just about work and a paycheck; Kenny and his wife, Misty, cared about our well-being. They were both there for me when I received my five-year and ten-year sobriety medallions, sitting on those stained chairs to cheer me on. He was a father to me, and I'll always be grateful to them for consistently checking in on us.

At the end of the day, I know the changes in the contract were a business decision for Kenny, and they just didn't happen to align with my plans. I didn't want to live with the constant anxiety of will-I-or-won't-I be able to make my payment each month.

I gave Kenny my two weeks' notice. I was ready to go out on my own now. My personal van was so rusty the guys would make fun of me. "Hey, Rory! When you drive around town, we see moms pulling their kids in close, scared you're gonna take off with 'em."

I didn't care. Because that van was mine. As I was driving down Twelfth Street one day, I slammed on the brakes in front of a laundromat, the same one I used to rest in when the shelter was packed. Right next to it, there was a small bait shop—a shed, really—with a "for sale" sign hanging on it. I tracked down the owners, a couple from Muskogee, Oklahoma.

"I know you're trying to sell it, and the second you do, I'll be out that month. Till then, can I rent it? At least you'll have some income coming your way. What do you say to a month-to-month lease?"

When they agreed, I turned the old bait shop into a working shed and slapped a small sign with "Rory's" on it. I even stuck a sticker with the logo on the side of my van. I'd asked one of the guys at AA, a graphic designer, to create one for me, and his blue crackled design has been part of my brand ever since. It was winter and I set up electric space heaters inside. It was just me and Miah, the boy who loved eagles, and maybe a helper when we could afford one. We worked off a cheap plastic folding table from Menards and ran sticky notes up and down the walls with details about upcoming jobs, color-coded for siding, roofing, and windows. We went around town, sticking annoying little "Rory's" signs in people's yards and on street corners to get the word out.

Sales took off, and I got an assistant. When she first started, without a phone line or computer, she'd field calls on my cell. If a client happened to ring and I picked up, I would tell them I needed to put them on a brief hold for my assistant and then quietly slide the phone to her. The guy on the other end never suspected she was two feet away from me inside our cramped office shed.

We kept subcontracting out roofing jobs and eventually did the same for siding. Miah and I focused all our energy on windows. He did the exterior work, bending and wrapping aluminum, while I handled the trim. The day I let him fully install a window all by himself, we celebrated. He'd come a long way.

Three years back, when I was sponsoring Miah and saw his commitment to stay clean, I rented out the basement of my Seventh Street house to him. Sabina and I stayed upstairs. At the time, he was working at Barnes & Noble over at Peace Plaza. I showed up one day and asked him, "Hey, you want to learn a trade? Something you can carry with you for life, something nobody can take from you?" His nod was the start to our lasting friendship. Every morning, when Miah would hear me shuffling around upstairs, he knew it was time to get up and get going. I taught him that it doesn't matter what your day is set to look like, you just gotta suit up and show up.

When I asked him to measure something out an inch and seven-eighths, he was confused. "Seven inches? Seventy-eight?"

So, we started at the beginning, and I taught him how to read a tape measure using a cheater tape with labels for every line. He followed me around, keeping things clean and his eyes open, always learning. Eventually, we got him his own set of tools, and I brought him onto the window crew with me at Rob's. Little by little, I built him up till he could install a window faster than I ever could.

One afternoon, Miah skidded to a stop alongside me on the road, and with a grin, he said, "Man, what's up, Rory? Now I'm driving your white truck. You got a dollar? 'Cause I got one." That became our running joke. We'd swap dollars as a reminder of where we'd come from. He'd leave a bill on my windshield, and I'd sneak one into his tool bucket. Jeremiah, who used to bug everyone as the "annoying little Indian kid who keeps asking for a cigarette and a dollar," now trains new guys into the window crew and is getting ready to buy his own house. He shows up and works hard. He's happy. He's on his way.

From our little shed that first summer, we worked ninety-six days, from sunrise to way past sunset. In those early days, I made it a point to visit every single jobsite. I wanted to say hi, shake hands, hold the baby, and pet the puppy. I'd personally tell them, "If you need anything, just let us know." I was all about providing top-notch customer service, even if that meant long hours, including Sundays. In between jobs, we'd walk a few blocks to the Pioneer Club, chat and sip coffee, and catch a breather.

Once, I overheard an old-timer tell their sponsee, "Why don't you get some goals? Fucking want something. You want your own place? Work every day, save up, and go get it. Now, you've got a reason to give a damn about tomorrow and stay clean."

I was reminded of my mission to leave behind all those times when I'd sit in my car, turn the key, and it wouldn't fucking start.

If working meant succeeding, I could do that. I'd done it before: I was once a scrawny, 105-pound addict, trudging through snow and hitchhiking from Hastings, up Highway 52, to Saint Paul, freezing my ass off while hunger tore away at me, all for a fucking hit of a twenty rock. Now, I just took that same energy and poured it into growing my business. Maybe I brought even more passion, trying to make up for all the lost years.

***

I spent a full year in that shed when I got a call. "Rory, we're ready to sell the bait shop and the laundromat as a package, if you're interested." I sat right up. It was the lady from Muskogee. Yes, I was interested, with all of my $6,500 in the bank and just a handful of jobs lined up. Despite the reality, I was all in with my Rory fire, my kick and snap, and I went after my dream.

On Mondays, Fridays, and weekends, I rocked my paint-stained "Rory's"-branded T-shirts and hoodies, grinding on jobsites. But come Tuesdays, Wednesdays, and Thursdays, I switched to a pressed button-down shirt from the left side of my closet and focused on sales. I added more and more jobs to the line of sticky notes, and in between, I would drive to different banks across town, applying for commercial loans. Months went by without a word. One afternoon, I stopped by West Bank, housed in a brand-new building with large-screen TVs, an interior lounge, and a rooftop terrace. I was in awe of the beautiful stonework and chandeliers, wondering how a bank could look like this.

When I walked in, I was greeted with a friendly, "Hey, Rory!" It was Mike Zinser. I had done a major kitchen remodel for him while I was still working for Kenny. Apparently, he was now the president of West Bank. I made my case: I had left Rob's Construction and had a business opportunity. I'd been in this line of work most of my life, and I just needed someone to give me a chance.

"Rory, let's see what we can do. We'll have an answer for you by Friday."

I filled out the necessary paperwork, sharing my financial information. And I anxiously waited. Even if I could buy the place, what the fuck was I going to do with it? They had taken most of the laundry equipment out and left behind large pieces of cracked sheet glass. Cisterns cut across the floor for the washing machine muck to drain. We'd have to fill them all in with cement. The walls needed scrubbing, framing, and insulation, and the entire flooring, bathroom, and utility room needed to be redone. The only thing worth saving was the ceiling with its large beams, but even they were rough to the touch and had paint spots, so that still needed work.

When the bank called with the news, "Rory, we want to work with you," I closed my eyes, my chest tight. It was a dream before, but now within reach, overwhelming doubt set in. I wasn't worried about the loan payments. I could still work out of the old bait shop and count on that regular stream of income. What pressed on me most was that West Bank was asking for 20 percent upfront. That was a ton of cash I didn't have, and I had to act quickly.

There was another bank across town that offered high-interest loans whenever I needed to buy large equipment. Fifteen thousand at a time. Apparently, I was a "gold member," one of just a few who had borrowed money and paid it off early. They said they could offer me their max. I combined that with my savings, and forty-five minutes before the closing, Lilly and I hurried to our bank to deposit a check I had just received from a big job. Then we raced over, and using every last dime, I wrote out a check for the full down payment for the property and handed it over to West Bank. My accounts were at zero.

After the closing, Lilly and I drove to the laundromat. I sat on the floor and cried. As I looked around, wiping my tears, I took in the nasty scene: Old dryers lined one wall, and a deep pit in the middle of the floor was full of lint and hair. The smell of moldy, wet rags hung around us. But, I thought, this was mine. I owned it. And it was beautiful. Just beautiful. I loved it. My wife stared at me, raising her eyebrows and scrunching her nose, before she softly said, "Okay, if this is what you truly believe in...okay." And I did.

I kept working out of the shed during the day, and in my spare time, evenings, and weekends, I'd head over to the laundromat. I'd Sheetrock a little, get a couple of windows done, work on the floors, and bring in plumbers and electricians. I worked, made a little money, and put it right back into the remodel—for two whole years. I didn't want to slap a bandage over the place. I wanted the fancy trim and expensive lighting. The look of a mini Bellagio. If this was going to be my home base, I wanted to give it all the love I had. One weekend, I got a shipment of forty boxes with parts for a massive desk. I assembled it one small piece after another.

One day at a time, one screw at a time, I built my dream.

***

After nearly three years since giving Kenny my two weeks' notice, the day finally came when I moved into the remodeled laundromat, leaving the shed with its folding table and sticky notes behind. I grew my business with these principles in mind:

Treat people right. Don't screw them. Be nice. If you fuck something up, fix it and make it right. And you're going to fuck up. It's construction. Or you're going to do something, and they won't like it. If it's within reason, change it. To me, that's the foundation of owning a business: just be good.

We grew our team to twelve employees, with more subcontractors on top of that. At peak, we had twenty-three people working at a single site. There was a crew on the roof, another installing siding, a deck getting built, someone gutting a bathroom, another renovating a kitchen, and new windows being installed. We were a small business, but we grew because I cared about my employees. I'd take time to learn about their lives outside of work, offering help where I could. You're going through a divorce? Want me to come over with my trailer to help you move? Or, are you getting along with your girlfriend okay? Because I just heard you screaming at your phone. They'd open up and share their stories with tears streaming down, and I'd listen.

I paid a good wage too. In many cases, fifty cents to a dollar more than a company twice our size. I had faith that we'd be good at what we did and profit. In the first year at the old bait shop, we grossed $70,000. The next year, my column of sticky notes grew so much it spilled off the Menards table, and we grossed around $250,000. Once we moved into the old laundromat, we hit the million-dollar mark and a thousand window installs. My best year surpassed $1.5 million.

I took the profits and learned how to invest in real estate. At peak, I owned seven rental properties—sixteen total doors, as they say in the business. A seven-plex, a duplex, a triplex, a couple of houses, and two commercial buildings—how am I even saying this? It still shocks me. Along the way, I gained a reputation in the county for taking a chance on men, women, and families in recovery, even those with criminal records, renting to them when no one else would. This was never my plan, but at one point, nearly all of my renters were in recovery. At times, I got burned on rent money, hearing promises like, "Hey, dude, I got you. Don't worry. I'll bring it to you, bruh, it's all good." Yet, two weeks later, the same dude would be sneaking around the back stairs, ducking and avoiding eye contact. I was a fucking sap. But I kept my focus on the 90 percent who made their payments and worked with the rest the best I could.

When Rory's started gaining momentum, Lilly and I made the decision to sell the Seventh Street house and then stumbled across an old farm for sale on the outskirts of Rochester. Massive trees overran the land, many of them dead. There was an old pig barn and a small gardening shed that reeked of bat urine. And the farmhouse itself had addition upon addition upon addition made over the years, all in different styles, with 1980s paneling. It needed a lot of work, but it was mine and I loved it.

People had been shocked when I bought my shack of a house on Seventh Street, and then shocked again with the run-down laundromat. Now, with the farmhouse, I told them to wait. Just wait. I see beauty in things before others do. Whether it's a house, a building, or a person. Maybe it's because of where I've been and what I've seen. But what makes a bad, or a less than, or a shitty impression on others doesn't affect me. I'm not in denial. I can imagine what the plumbing looks like, or I can smell the alcohol on someone's breath, just like anyone else. But for me, it's as if I'm swimming in the ocean, darkness all around, and when I push against the force of the water and propel my body forward, I can see the beginnings of color just beyond. That tiny glimpse of color is what I focus on.

I took down seventy-seven box elder, Dutch elm, and ashford trees on our new property. When the chainsaw nicked my thigh, I duct-taped it and kept going. Now, our home has a clear view of the sunrise and the flowing Zumbro River just behind it. In the spring, the whole bank fills with bluebells.

If you were to see my home, you'd think we were getting ready to move. The kitchen counters are clear of appliances. There's minimal furniture. I live and move with such high energy that to be calm in my own home, it needs to look as if I've just finished it. I built a she-shed for Lilly so she could have a space of her own to spread out her arts and crafts, and a quiet place to read and paint, with throw pillows and potted succulents crowded around her.

In the six years we've lived here, Lilly and I have hosted at least two weddings every summer in our backyard. We cover the windows of the she-shed for the bride to get ready. My assistant at Rory's as well as my ex-girlfriend Viola's daughter, Jordan, both walked down the aisle at my home. We hold the after-party in our larger shed with a DJ stand I custom-built with changing lights. I always tell the bride and groom that my gift to them will be a fireworks show. I love fireworks, and really, the wedding event is just an excuse to cross state lines and get the most monstrous ones. I pile up boxes in the truck till every inch is covered. I live for the finale and the explosion of colors—a grand celebration of life.

When I got sick with cancer and slowly downsized my business and properties, I had time on my hands and saw a chance to renovate the old farmhouse itself. I didn't want to die in a hospital. If I had to go, I wanted it to be in my bedroom, the way I envisioned it. I'd worked on so many people's homes; it was my turn now. I ripped out the flooring and gutted the entire kitchen and bathrooms. Lilly and I lived in our basement for months while I worked. Every day, she'd come home and ask, "What are you doing?" The demo got worse and worse, but I told her to trust me, that this was my profession. There was a Sheetrock guy coming in ten minutes, or tapers scheduled for Friday, or we had to look at paint samples in an hour. It kept my mind busy and left me no time to feel sick.

Some of the guys from Rory's would come over to help. I saw they worried about me, but they all knew I'd never give an excuse to not work. Besides the day of my ablation surgery to destroy the tumor tissue on my spine, I never missed a day. (And that was only because I was under anesthesia on the surgery table.) Throughout all the treatments—radiation, chemo, immunotherapy—I would still show up at work with a walker, get the crews started, and sit in my office chair. In between, I'd shuffle to the bathroom when vomit would creep up. I thought, why wouldn't I keep working? If I didn't, it would be like giving up. So I propped myself in that chair at Rory's every single day.

With the effects of chemo, I may have mismeasured a window or two in the farmhouse. Off by just a little bit. I could hear them tease, "Who measured these? Rory?" I was still one of the guys. That never changed.

When all of the rooms finally came together in perfect harmony—freshly painted gray walls with white trim, a sleek quartz countertop, luxury vinyl plank flooring, brand-new cabinetry, and a matching subway tile backsplash—Lilly squealed, "Oh, my God! I didn't know you could do this!"

"Honey, what do you think I've been doing for the past fifteen years?" We joked, but what I didn't tell her was that I wanted to leave her a home in good condition, one that she could sell when I was gone.

Rory with Jeremiah (right)

Rory's Home Improvement

YOU BOPPING YOUR HEAD UP
AND DOWN AGAIN? WHY DON'T
YOU LOOK *AT* PEOPLE?

When Sabina came to live with me, we'd celebrate "Chip Night" every so often on Saturday nights at the Pioneer Club. For a while, we heard, "So, this next person, Joe, is six months sober and will be receiving a pin from…Rory" and, "This next person, Matthew, will be getting his seven-month pin from… Rory." At times, I'd taken on so many sponsees that it would just be me up there, handing out chips.

The longer I stayed sober, the more guys I sponsored. I was up to working with eight men at once and going to meetings five nights a week. At that point in my life, I needed to talk to others in recovery; with any time off, I believed I would have gotten high again. For recovery to work, they always say you have to give it away to keep it. As I mentored sponsees, our conversations held me accountable. I was saying things that were going in my ear too when I needed a reminder later. No one else was pointing fingers and telling me what to change. I'd recognize my own hypocrisy: Had I been too focused on money lately too? Getting too close to temptations? Is that the man I wanted to be? Because if I was telling my guys one thing and then finding the nearest bar, that's a tough one for anyone to live with and still look themselves in the eye. So, I should say: the longer I stayed sober, the more guys I sponsored, and the more guys I sponsored, the longer I stayed sober.

Indian Mike once told me, "Hey, Rory, whatcha bopping your head up and down for? You always looking up and down at everyone. You either look at them, like they're way down to the ground, like they're a piece of shit. Or you look up at the guy with the convertible and a hot chick up front. Why don't you start looking *at* people, eye to eye, then maybe your neck won't hurt so much."

He said the best way to understand and communicate with anyone in this world was to stay level. "You need to…" and "You always…" and "You never…" Don't fucking use those words. I should know, because whenever people talked to me like that, I developed an automatic ability to just shut off the noise. You don't fucking know me and what I've been through, and how are you any better? You could be talking to me, and I wouldn't hear a word you're saying because I'm a fucking professional and have mastered that ability. I know it's common to say "I'm his sponsor," or, "He's my sponsee," but right away that language creates a power dynamic. No, we're all in this together, and if my messages don't reach them, they'll stop reaching me.

***

A year or two before I got diagnosed with cancer, I came into Rory's early one morning and walked around the building, picking up stray trash and loading construction equipment for that day. Between the wooden fence and the tree line, where the weeds had taken over, I sensed movement. I was surprised to see a young guy in his twenties sit straight up in a hammock, looking worried. He quickly said, "Hey, sorry, man. I'll get out of here as soon as I can."

"No, it's okay," I assured him. "What's your name? Can I talk to you for a second? You don't have to leave, alright? You're fine here." I noticed a needle on the ground and an open box of Cheerios that was probably stale. "Have you eaten today? You hungry? Let's go to Kwik Trip across the street and I'll get you something."

"No, no. I'm fine. I'm good."

I insisted, and as we walked over to the gas station, I continued, "Listen, if the cops come, you tell them that Rory—the name on that sign right there—gave you permission to be here. And if there's any trouble, they can come talk to me. You're safe here."

The next day, I told Miah that we had one of us back there. We found his hammock, but the kid was gone. Eventually, I cut it down from the trees and threw it away.

A couple of years later, I received an invitation to the grand opening of The Landing, a place that serves the homeless community in Rochester. Lilly and I were mingling and shaking hands when a guy walked up to me with a friendly, "Hey, Rory!"

"Heeeey!" I stalled and raised an eyebrow at Lilly because I couldn't quite place him—clean-cut, well-dressed, and handsome. He must have noticed our confusion because he continued, "You probably don't remember me, but I know who you are."

I let out a nervous laugh because this could go one of two ways.

"I was sleeping behind your business in the woods. You took me to get something to eat and treated me like a human being. What you did that day helped change my life."

We were all getting choked up. I wanted to say, "No, I didn't recognize you, dude. You were shooting up meth with dirt on your face, and frankly, you smelled." The man standing in front of me now, with his short hair and smiling eyes, could have been mistaken for a Mercedes dealer.

His name was Tyler, and he had left his hammock behind because he got arrested that same night. When I met him, he'd been living on the streets for four years. Usually, he'd wake up at sunrise, pack up, and be gone before anyone noticed. But on that particular night, he'd been up for a couple of days, exhausted from trying to survive. I'd startled him awake, and when I approached, he assumed I'd yell at him or call the cops. But it was the opposite.

Lilly and I were openly crying now as Tyler continued, "When I was homeless, I felt isolated, out of place, unwanted—like an eyesore. If I walked into Hyvee Barlow in the middle of February, not to steal groceries or anything, but just to warm up in the entryway for a few minutes…they'd kick me out just by looking at me. It broke me down to the point where it was easier to keep my head down than to keep it up. I mean, I'd literally walk with my head down on the sidewalk. That's when you lose hope, you know?

"When I met you, I had a lot of pride, and it took time to accept your help. But over a hot breakfast, you asked me my name and shared a bit of your story. We connected. You gained my trust, and that made my ears open up to your words. Those select few people who cross your path and don't judge you but just offer words of encouragement, like you did, Rory…they're the ones who kept me going for four years.

"I ended up in jail that night. I'd been running from a warrant; stealing meals from gas stations finally caught up to me. I had a lot of time to think in that cell, and I kept spinning your words around, how you were in my shoes once and made it out. You told me, 'Life is hard, but surviving is even harder. If you can survive this, and you have been, then you can find a better life.'

"When you've been outside of society for so long, it takes some convincing to accept help. Did I want to get sober? I did, but a part of me believed that I didn't deserve to get sober because I was homeless. And the only future I could see was my next step: how would I get my next meal, how would I stay warm? Truly, the only way I survived those four years was by staying addicted and numbing the pain. Using became a survival tactic, but I wanted to break free, like you had. The next day, I asked to go to treatment instead of serving my jail time. In my mind, I was meant to meet you that day. I've been waiting to thank you ever since."

He was now a peer recovery specialist at a local treatment center and worked at The Landing too. Lilly and I hugged Tyler goodbye, and I whispered to him, "I owe you a hammock, my friend."

The simplicity of that moment when we met is what makes it so big. I didn't really know him, and he didn't know me. It wasn't about what either of us had. I didn't hand him a ten-dollar bill. That's not helping; that's feeding an addiction. I could see he was hungry. So I walked alongside him to get a bite to eat, and we talked. I chose my words from what I would've wanted to hear when I was in his shoes. I rarely ask, "How's it going?" That's like when you're at a funeral and you hear people whisper, "How are you holding up?" The moment they do, the person starts crying. Of course, they're feeling shitty. They just lost somebody. Instead, how about this: "If you need anything, let us know." And that's it. Stop.

To someone with an addiction, "How are you doing?" quickly spirals into "What are you doing? What's wrong with you? Why did you do that?" All these things people sit and yell at us. You just reminded them of everything that's going wrong in their lives.

So, right away, they withdraw and pull back from you. Instead, when I see someone who seems broken, and if it feels right, I ask, "Hey, do you want a cup of coffee? What are you doing tonight? Want to get something to eat?" That's how genuine and honest communication starts. It's not about how I'm coming in to save you.

Men who have been tormented, been through hell, have no hope, and can't trust another man or woman have allowed me into their hearts, into their personal lives, and into their pasts. They've shared their nightmares and resentments, things they've never revealed to anyone before. As their sponsor, I sit and listen, but it weighs on me. What happens to them isn't something I can just brush off. I can't just say, "Good luck, little birdie." I worry about them. Their struggles become my own—and it's an honor because I was *invited* behind their wall. They become like family to me, so much a part of who I am.

My experience on the streets shaped the way I treated Tyler. I could see what was truly beneath his "I'm fine, I'm good" act. And that helped change this guy's life. Knowing this gives purpose to all the pain and suffering I've endured. This is why nothing I've been through can ever bother me too much. It led me to these people and the conversations we've shared. I'd go through it all again because these connections are better than any paycheck. It's the good stuff in life.

That's why I miss helping out at AA. I miss the meetings and guiding meditations. But when I started chemo, I just didn't have the energy to be around other people. I'd go into work, and by noon, without the same lung capacity and stamina, I'd be wiped and ready for a nap. Lately, getting involved again in the recovery community has been on my mind, how I'd like to ground myself where it all started for me. I'm not like everyone else. I'm off a little bit—a weirdo, goofy, a wiggler. I think that may be the greatest gift of all because when I say that it's never too late for anyone to change, no matter what they've done, people believe me. They're not looking up at me with, "Yes, sir, I'll try to do that. I'll try not to use. I'll be better and go to school, and then maybe I can be a good person like you who's waaaaay up there, out of reach, distant from me, who I can't get near." Instead, I'm right there, sitting across from them, someone they can reach out and touch, making them think, "Maybe I *can* do this."

When life gets good and you start making money, it's easy to become too tall. Sometimes, when I'm driving, I'll catch myself thinking, "You know what the neighbor needs to do?" or, "If her husband would just..." I've got to be careful with that language. I don't know that journey of *if he would just...* I can only share what worked for me and hope they can find what they need. They might, or they might not. But it's when people in recovery are doing well that they have to stay the most humble. Whenever I connect with a person, eye to eye, I feel the rightness in my bones. But when I'm talking like this, with judgment, that feeling is far away.

Being around other guys in recovery every day reminds me of where I came from, how I could be back there in a minute, and that puts me right where I belong. I want to get back to speaking to students too, like at the ALC. Every time I come out there, the students write me letters that I read and toss. I worry about holding on to them because I know I'll read them again and again and think, "Oh, look at what these kids said about *me*." I can't do that. Because the second I get there, I grow wings. Indian Mike taught me, "Ego stands for Edging God Out." It becomes about me—look at me and look at what I did. No, I've got to stay with my two feet on the ground.

GOT A CHOICE TO MAKE? JUST PLAY THE STORY OUT.

Whenever I come across a man with an addiction who insists, "I don't have a choice," I say, "Actually, we do. We have a choice before that first hit, when we're still sober. We have a choice to pick up this rock or buy that bottle of Bacardi Rum with a liter of cola. But once we start using, that choice is ripped away by the effects on our mind, body, and spirit. So now, I *need* to get money because I *need* to get high to keep going. You see, once it's inside me, I use because I fucking have to. It's not about having fun anymore."

***

Steve hasn't had a drink in almost fifteen years and still goes to meetings three times a week to keep from picking up again. When I met him, he was a mouthy complainer—life was out to get him. But when people think of him now, they see his bright smile and how you can almost see his wheels turning before he speaks. Once, he openly wondered what would happen if he had just one drink.

A friend of ours quickly chimed in, saying, "Play the whole story out. Don't just stop the movie at 'what's going to happen if I take this one drink.' Play it all the way through."

The whole story would go like this: If Steve had that one glass, he wouldn't stop. He'd keep drinking till he passed out or blacked out or ran out. Eventually, he'd lose his wife, his kids, and his home. There was a time when staying sober for even a week seemed impossible to him. That time had brought him to his knees, begging for help in his tiny basement apartment. These days, he worries about which bathroom sink fixture would look nicer in the four-bedroom home he owns. Today, he would know what it was like to lose if he ever chose to pick up a drug or drink again, and if he loses what he has today, he says you might as well put him in the gutter. The end.

When a sponsee would call me and share their plans for the night, plans that included barhopping, I could have gently said, "Well, you know, being as how you're so early in recovery, it would be best if you just hung out at home tonight. I'm just suggesting this to you. Take care of yourself, and I'll see you in a couple of days." The loving, patient, and tolerant approach worked with some, but I quickly learned that most were desperate for someone to be real with them about how things would *actually* go. I became a fucking asshole when I needed to be:

"Really? You actually think it's a good idea to drive to see a band in a place full of girls and booze, where they're selling fucking dope in the back? You're two weeks sober, you're pissed, you're not fucking happy with your job, your wife just left you, and you think you're just gonna hang out? This is what you're calling to tell me? Then you're calling the wrong dude. That's the dumbest fucking idea I've ever heard. At *this* moment in your life. You have no stability, no strength to pull from, you have an addiction, and you're dropping in the middle of a war zone by yourself with no fucking weapon? You're gonna lose. You're wasting my time, and especially, you're wasting yours. Because I'm fine. I'm going to have a happy fucking life tomorrow. Everything's going to be just great. And you're going to fuck up everything you've been fighting for just to go down to some bar? No. Tonight, you're not going out to watch your friends play at the bar, thinking you'll be fine. You're going to sit your ass down at a meeting, and then go fucking home to bed. Check yourself."

He'd get the point. "Okay, dude, okay, just calm down. Can you pick me up on your way to the Pioneer Club?" And just like that, his story was to be continued...

***

Early on in my relationship with Lilly, I set the condition that if she used again, I wouldn't be with her. That's how we live today. If one of us relapses, we'll leave each other for good.

Lilly started drinking at the age of fourteen, and her very first time, she drank to blackout. The switch inside flipped on. She stumbled down a stairwell with a glass in her hand. When she woke up, it was in a hospital room getting her hand stitched up while her dad sat beside her, sobbing. For the next eight years, her life became a cycle of late-night parties and visits to the ER for acute alcohol intoxication.

A blood alcohol content level of more than a .25 is considered life-threatening. Most people would pass out and run the risk of choking on their own vomit. But during one ER visit, Lilly was still walking and talking at a .25 level. Her tolerance was just that high. She shouted at a young resident, "Let me out of here! Can't you see, I'm fine?!"

He stayed firm. "I could lose my medical license if I let you walk out of here right now. It could be fatal."

After her seventeenth trip to the ER, Lilly's dad told social workers, "No more. I can't do this. I don't want her in an apartment by herself. She's going to kill herself. And she can't come back home till she gets help." By that time, Lilly knew all of the regulars going in and out of detox and would wave goodbye to them as if they were old friends.

She dropped out of college and was given a court-ordered stay of commitment when she voluntarily checked herself into a six-month inpatient treatment program. In her last week, she went to a liquor store and bought a bottle of vodka. When her sponsor eventually found her, she was completely incapacitated and had passed out drunk, lying in her own vomit. Her social workers petitioned for her to be placed on another six-month stay of commitment, with the understanding that if she drank again or left treatment, she would be committed against her will.

That's when she started at Liberalis, a semi-locked, state-funded treatment facility that used to be an old nursing home. She was the only woman under thirty and the only one who burned for alcohol; the others were hooked on heroin and meth, and it scared the shit out of her. They could say what the food was like in four different facilities across the state. She played the story out, and that moment opened Lilly's eyes to what her future would be if things didn't change: treatment centers would become hotels.

In March 2013, Lilly was transferred to Pathways in Rochester, where she could live sober with support. She often thought back to the summer before her senior year of college when she worked for a woman named Ann as a nanny for her daughter, Margie. Lilly had stolen an expensive blouse from Ann's closet, and even though she put it back three days later, she thinks Ann knew. Because the next day, Lilly saw a new message written in blue marker on the whiteboard above Margie's desk: "You are what you do, not what you did."

When Lilly successfully completed her stay at the halfway house, she got her own apartment. One of the first things she did was to write that affirmation on a bright pink sticky note and pin it to her bulletin board: *You are what you do, not what you did.* She was still fragile, but the note was a reminder that she had the potential for a good life—for a fresh start to a different story, and that excited her. When we met, she was in a stable routine of waitressing, taking each day as it came, and staying sober.

Back when she had withdrawn from Lawrence University, Lilly had been pursuing a bachelor's degree in English and history. In 2020, she made the decision to go back to school and took one class per semester toward her remaining credits. It was a challenging two years of juggling twenty-five-page papers, work, and life with me. Being the oldest student was daunting, but after eleven years since she'd first enrolled in college, she did it. She walked across the stage at the US Bank Stadium to receive her diploma, with her parents in the audience.

Lilly and I both know that our life is beyond what we ever dreamed. The only way we can fuck this story up now is if we start using.

I don't think I could have stayed sober if I'd married someone who could drink. When your significant other is coming home slightly tipsy from a girls' night on a Friday while you're trying to be sober, that can be tough. I don't trust myself enough. I'd start missing that and would want to give her company and give in to my addiction. I can even picture the routine we'd fall into: We'd get up to go to work to get money to come home and have a drink. A vicious cycle that would inevitably end with an ex-wife and a kid who won't talk to me, while I sit alone on the couch wondering what the hell happened.

At the end of the road, there's jail, institutions, or death. And I've been around. I've been locked up in Dakota County, Hennepin County, Ramsey County, Scott County, Olmsted County... I've been in treatment in Pine Shores, Hastings, Red Wing, and Rochester. So how many times could I keep rolling the dice and get away with it?

Some guys will tell me, "Rory, I know I have a problem, but..." They might add, "but I think I can be a social drinker," or, "but I can do it only on the weekends," or, "but this one time won't hurt." Maybe *they* can, but for me, there's no gray area. For me, recovery means either I'm using or I'm not. I've been sober since 2005, but I live every day knowing that with just one drink, I could lose it all. One Bacardi Coke would turn into three and I'd be on my way to the Twin Cities to ask the working girls where I can get some rock. It doesn't matter what state I'm in or what country; I could find the right part of town and figure the rest out. I've harnessed and groomed a special power to walk into any bar and pick out the addict. I can find dope just by looking at people. All the odds are stacked against me. Not him, not him, not him either. Okay, there we go. "Hey, what's up man? What you up to?" Five minutes later, I'd be riding shotgun, headed to his trusted dealer.

Early in our relationship, when Lilly worked the patio at the Canadian Honker and served drinks, there were moments when she thought, "These people can sit here and drink on a summer night, like normal. It sucks." And once, while we were traveling, I casually mentioned how good the cocaine must be here. She was quick to reply, "Well, if you find out, you know I'll leave you here."

Not everyone has this switch inside them. It's crack for me. It might be Xanax, fentanyl, porn, or attention from men or women for you. Some don't have any switch, and some just don't know— thank goodness, and I hope you don't find out. But if you have the kind of switch that I do for something…you understand me. We have to think twice, or maybe a hundred times, because it might start with a little weed, but before long, we'll have a rum and Coke in one hand and a crack pipe in the other. Personally, I know I can't ever choose to touch these again because I've seen my story played out if I do. I've seen it with my best friend, Johnny, and my brother, David.

***

Back when I was living in Hastings and running my own dope house, Cindy was my meth dealer. One evening, she brought her boyfriend along with her. In walked Johnny, my outgoing, breakdancing best friend from when we were kids. Back then, we bought cheap radios and splashed paint all over them for the Excelsior Arts Festival in Minnetonka, Minnesota. We spread cardboard across the ground, blasted out Grandmaster Flash, and danced our hearts out. We called ourselves the Lake Breakers, and wore black parachute pants with zippers all over and baggy, puffy coats. We'd spin around the ground in a helicopter move, hold out our hats, and people would throw in money.

I had a lot of firsts with Johnny. We bought hash together, squeezed it into a pancake, and smoked it under a bridge. Later, under the same bridge, I got to second base with a girl, and on the other end, he did too. Every girl liked him. He would flip his hair back with a shake of his head, and they would just swoon over his caramel brown eyes.

Now, inside my dope house, Johnny sat in my La-Z-Boy recliner and whispered, "Don't judge me for this." I watched as he stuck a needle in his arm. Heroin. Cindy walked over with a wet rag and a bucket. He threw up into it, and she gently cooled his forehead with the damp cloth, explaining, "We do this so he can wake up in the morning." They had the routine down.

A few months later, Johnny's mom called me. "Rory, we need to talk. Can you sit down?" Johnny had heroin on him when cops were chasing him down I-35W in Minneapolis. He was on his motorcycle and had always outrun them before. This time, they were too close, so he swallowed the whole bag. He made it home and took ipecac to vomit up the drugs. When Cindy came out of the shower, he was gone, dead on the couch.

***

When I moved back home with Dad to start culinary school, my brother, David, stayed back in Florida. That's where he died in 2009. At the age of thirty-nine. Growing up, he and I were each other's shadows, and with just a year's difference between us, people often confused us for twins. We looked out for each other. He let me tag along with his friends, and when he just couldn't get the Hebrew down, we had a double bar mitzvah so I could help with the Torah readings. I spoke the long prayers while he took the shortest ones.

He never liked sitting in school all day, but like my older brothers who were captains of the swim team, David thrived in the pool. In competitions, I might swim the 100-meter breaststroke, but David had the stamina for twenty fucking laps and could go longer, too. He loved the butterfly stroke, one of the toughest to master. You had to keep just the right rhythm, a balance of power and grace.

His roommate said he hung himself. When I got the call, my brothers and I flew down, rented a boat, and sprinkled his ashes in the waters near Destin, Florida. We found his trailer, and when we opened the door, roaches scattered away. Tim said he wouldn't have let his dog live there. Blankets hung from the ceiling to separate the living room from the bedroom, and an extension cord ran from the neighbor's trailer to power the AC. David didn't have anything to his name. At his funeral, a few friends brought photos, and Tim noticed that David wore the same shirt in many of them. He just had the one fancy shirt.

We were told that David had looped an electrical cord through the fan and tied it around his neck. Part of me wondered how a rotted ceiling could have held his weight, that maybe something else had gone down. Police had investigated, but he was a dead addict in a wrecked trailer in one of the roughest parts of the city. No witnesses? Okay. Call the family. Case closed. I just couldn't accept his suicide.

What hurt me most was that, around the time David died, when he was living in squalor, I was finally finding some stability in my own life. I had my home on Seventh Street and a job at Rob's Construction that I had been loyal to for years. I wanted to bring David here, to live with me and to help him find work. So when I got that call—"David was found dead"—I parked my car on the side of the road, leaned against the passenger side door, and sobbed. One agonizing thought hammered inside me: what if I'd gotten down there in time?

It took awhile, but a few months ago, I finally threw away all the records from the investigation because I knew it wouldn't change a thing. I know the life David was living in his broken-down trailer with alcohol, drugs, and prostitutes; it was the same life that I lived for a long time. But I've accepted I can't carry that guilt. His choices don't have anything to do with me. I'd been holding on to David's shark-tooth necklace, and when I was ready, I passed it on to Steve, telling him, "You're my brother now." And I kept living forward.

Rory's brother, David

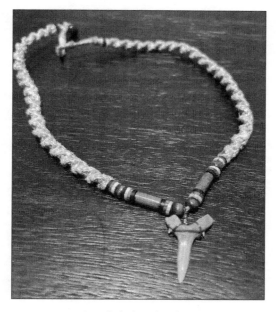

David's shark-tooth necklace

KEEP YOUR SIDE OF
THE STREET CLEAN

Sometimes, when we have too much time alone to think, our minds can get stuck on past wrongs. When I met Steve, he and his ex-wife could never see eye to eye. They would scream insults back and forth from different states, she in South Dakota and he in Minnesota. I'd heard enough.

"Why don't you give her some credit? Is your son fed? (Yes.) Does he have clothes to wear? (Yes.) Does he have a roof over his head? (Yes.) Then quit your bitching about her. Just quit it. Knock it off. You're not solving anything. She's a great mom. In fact, why don't you say she's a great mom?"

I made him say it.

Again.

And again.

And then he made amends in person. (Her jaw was on the floor.)

Without drugs and alcohol to numb the hurt anymore, Steve was sitting in so much past hate that he had missed the fact that their son's basic needs were being met. In the big picture, she was doing her job as a mother and his son was well taken care of. And they were fighting over whether he could go see some movie? Come on.

Resentment, more than anything else, destroys people who struggle with addiction—not divorce, not losing your business, not the wife taking the kids and leaving you. All of that can happen and you might still be okay, but if you're holding on to resentment and you're angry? That's what's going to kill you. We've all felt it festering, growing bigger inside us; its roots could be years old, and we say, "Remember three years ago when you…" For three years, we've held on to it. The person listening is left wondering, "What…? When…? What are you even talking about?"

"You know! Three years ago! On November 17 at 2:43 p.m. How don't you remember?!"

I'm joking, but as someone with a substance problem, if we don't clean this up right now, it *will* be our end. It's not about complete forgiveness. Sometimes, we just have to consider how we can best move forward without being chained to our anger. It might take a person on the outside to jar us out of our one-track thinking of how we were wronged. Maybe prompt us to see all sides, maybe own up to our part, maybe consider—what is it finally time to let go of? When Steve made amends to his ex-wife, their relationship began to change. She didn't have to be on guard during every conversation, and as she softened, he maintained course too.

***

After the SuperAmerica robbery in 2001, it was time to make amends and face the people I had hurt. My sponsor at the time,

Glen, was working through the steps with me, and I shared that when I was living on the streets in Minneapolis, Aunt Sylvia wasn't the only one I had lied to and extorted money from.

Stan was a dishwasher at the 510 where I'd been working as a sous-chef after Dad died. He had a mental disability, and everyone would look out for him. He lived in a low-income high-rise, and we would take turns picking him up for work and dropping him off afterward.

By the time I was living out of my car, I was out of cash. I was downtown smoking crack one day, soaked and chilled from the rain, and found myself near Stan's place. I buzzed various combinations of numbers at the entrance till I finally heard his voice on the intercom.

"Who's there? Rory?! Yeah, come on up!"

I cut through the small talk and gave Stan the same story about my sad car troubles that I'd given Aunt Sylvia. He immediately offered, "I only have $120 to my name till I get paid again, but I'll give it all to you if you need it, Rory."

As I rode the elevator down, I knew I was a piece of shit. Sixty bucks would have been enough, but Stan was so innocent and honest that he'd told me exactly how much he had. And I took every last fucking dime. But a hit of crack did its job, and I quickly forgot what I'd done to get it. It wasn't until Glen forced me to pause long enough to think about who I needed to make things right with that I remembered Stan. And with that, the truth of who I was smacked me in the face. Tears were streaming down my face, when Glen repeated: *Holding on to this will kill you.*

So, seven years after the fact, I was ready to make things right. On the drive from Rochester to the 510 in Minneapolis to find Stan, I relived that scene in his apartment over and over again. It was as bad as someone stealing a wallet from a ninety-year-old guy with a walker who had no chance of fighting back. When I got to the restaurant, I learned the owner's son was running the place now. He told me they still looked out for Stan and helped him with his bills. I wrote a check for two or three times the amount I'd taken, and told them, "He'll know what it's for," as I handed it over. Then I sat in my beat-up truck from Rob's and bawled my eyes out.

Some people may think back on something they said or did that hurt another person and try to brush it off as no big deal now. But trust me, it's never really small. It's always sitting on your mind, maybe in the way back, but it'll lurk there till the day you face it.

In 2019, a year before I was diagnosed with cancer, I was moved to organize a family get-together with Tim's help. It had been over two decades since I'd seen any of my extended family, and I wanted to let them know that for all those years I wasn't around, I came out okay; I was here now.

We met at Buca di Beppo, an Italian restaurant in downtown Minneapolis. We got there early, Lilly and I. Too early. I'd changed shirts twice and tried out a couple of different chairs before finally settling on one. I couldn't get comfortable until my family started rolling in. I'd missed them. I'd played ping-pong with these same cousins growing up, and now I felt their absence from my life even more as I took in their aged faces, over twenty years later. I greeted them, their spouses, and their children with hugs. But when Jimmy, Aunt Sylvia's son, showed up, I needed a moment.

When we were young, our entire Jewish family had watched me excel at school and later as the sous-chef at the 510, the finest restaurant in the whole state. They saw me proudly wearing my chef's hat and coat, with my name and credentials embroidered on them. They would say, "Jimmy's been doing so well since taking over the family business, and we know Rory's going to be just as successful. We're so proud."

Seeing Jimmy made my knees buckle. I'd been ashamed for so long. I knew the fall from grace into addiction. But how do you do the reverse? How do you come back from addiction into grace and still look people in the eye? It sucks. And it's hard. My family reassured me, saying, "It's okay. We're glad to see you doing well now," but they hadn't allowed me to do my part in owning up to my past.

I had sunk so low, smoking from a glass pipe in the dirt, buddying up with prostitutes in the most squalid of places, just to get a dollar for a hit of something you could melt on a piece of cigarette ash. Something I would do anything for. Something that I tried to lie to *you* for. That I did lie to *your mother* for. I imagined all those years my cousins were sharing stories about their kids' extracurriculars and their own career accomplishments, while my older brothers were fielding questions about my whereabouts. "We think he's back in jail. He's hooked on crack, maybe you've heard." Now, to be able to look at someone I loved and respected, to look at him with integrity and honor and say, "Hey, how's it going?" I'm a fucking good actor, but I'm not that good. Seeing Jimmy walk in, even when I think of it now, it still breaks me.

Both Mom and Dad were gone, and Aunt Sylvia too. Maybe that's part of the reason why this gathering meant so much to me. I could never make things right with them, but at least I could with the people in that room. That evening, I'd walked in with the pressure to make an impression, with Lilly's Mercedes parked out front and her designer purse. But I only felt my shame start to fade away when I privately approached each of my cousins and said I was sorry. Jimmy whispered back, "Your mom and dad would be proud of you. I hope you know that."

That night lifted a burden I had carried for so long. It helped me continue to where I am today.

***

It's often easier to use and numb than to confront resentments or seek forgiveness. When my guys share their stories with me, I've taken on the role of both sponsor and private investigator quite a few times. The source of hurt often goes way back. When my friend, Dale, was younger, he was arrested for conspiracy to manufacture meth and sentenced to six years in prison. He woke up to the jailer telling him he had visitors, and his three sisters walked in. He felt their disappointment in him to his core. Fifteen years later, he was holed away with thoughts of suicide as his last resort. I did some digging, and when I told him we were going on a road trip to see his sister, he asked, "Which one?"

I replied, "All of them."

One by one, we met them, and his mom too, who he hadn't spoken with in eight years. Some talked; others just listened, giving Dale an opportunity to make amends. How he'd pushed people away, grown distant, and isolated himself. He was sorry and wanted to do better. We stopped at his dad's gravesite too. Years' worth of resentment and anger and ego dissipated in eight hours.

To keep my guys moving forward in their journeys—and to remind myself too—I tell them: "If you're holding on to resentment or if you've made a mistake, clean it up. Keep your side of the street clean." It's just one more thing that keeps you down, hunched over. When you make things right, you can stand a little straighter and move on.

Rory (left) and Dale (right)

HOW WILL YOU SPEND THE TIME YOU'VE GOT LEFT?

In April 2020, my back started acting up. When I was a kid, they had warned me that one day, with my scoliosis, my back might get so bad that I wouldn't be able to work anymore. They gave my mom the option to put a rod up my spine but it came with a risk of paralysis. She didn't want to take that chance.

I was used to back pain, but this time, I was coughing up blood. The guys at work saw me hacking up phlegm with streaks of red and said, "Dude, that looks serious. You should go get it checked out."

"Nah. Let's get back to work."

"Well, don't you wanna—" *No.*

"Okay, but maybe you should just—" *No.*

I'm sorry, man, but for most of my life, as long as I could sit and stand, I never went near a doctor because the bills would pour in. Back when Sabina lived with me and we didn't have insurance yet, I'd take her in for appointments and shots; it took me years to pay off those bills. They'd threaten me with letters, making me afraid to step foot in a hospital. Unless you have to, you don't go, especially as a single father. I'd trained myself that way. Even now, with Lilly's insurance covering me, I was still reluctant just thinking about the co-pay.

For six months, I lived on Tylenol and Motrin to dull the pain. One morning, it took me twenty minutes just to get dressed while sitting in a chair. I'd been complaining about the pain all along, but Lilly had heard enough. She told me she couldn't help me till I helped myself and got it checked out. I told myself I was old. And I smoked back in the day. And I worked construction for years, breathing in dust. I kept blowing it off. Maybe I just didn't want to know how bad it was.

When I finally went in, the doctor said it might be ulcers. I went through an upper endoscopy procedure where they put a thin tube down my throat to look at my insides. Everything was clear. But later that evening, I could hardly stand and coughed up blood again. Lilly drove me to the emergency room and the doctor ordered X-rays of my chest and back. Again, all clear.

That's when Lilly called up her doctor friend, who advised, "You tell Rory to get back in there and demand a CT scan. If he's spitting up blood, go back in there. Now." This time, I let Lilly do the talking. We sat in the waiting room for the results.

I was told, "Mr. Londer, we're seeing something in the scan, but we're not the ones who interpret them. We want to keep you overnight, and a specialist will be here in the morning to speak to you."

They led me to a hospital room and I jumped onto the bed. I thought, I could get used to this, with nurses and aides asking me what I needed every half hour. "Would you like some more soup? How about hot tea?" Why yes, yes I would. When I put my gown on backward, the nurse just laughed. At this point, they'd tested and examined every part of my body; there was no shame there anymore. I bopped around the room with my ass peeking out. This was the state of my mind. I wasn't used to hospitals, and I thought it was just an ulcer they had missed.

The next morning, the doctor came in with a folding chair under each arm. Three more followed. One sat at the edge of my bed, two on my left, and one on my right. I looked at them and wanted to say, "Get the fuck outta here." I didn't want to hear it.

"Mr. Londer, we're here to discuss a very serious matter." I felt the ground shift under me. I was already falling through.

"Let me just call my wife." It was April 24, 2020, and the coronavirus pandemic was raging around the world. No visitors were allowed. With shaky hands, I managed a video call and held it up so Lilly could hear.

"Mr. Londer, we've reviewed your CT scans. You have an aggressive cancer that has spread to multiple areas of your body. You have a tumor on your spine, specifically on your T11 vertebrae, which explains your back pain. You have tumors on your pelvis and lung. There's also a tumor on your heart that's putting pressure on your trachea and affecting your oxygen flow. We want you to hear this from all of us right now: we're going to fight this, and we want you to fight with us."

Life as I knew it changed. Whatever had irritated me that week or bothered me at work, none of it mattered. Unwashed dishes in the sink. Charter overcharging for the internet. All those concerns suddenly meant nothing. When Lilly's doctor friend called to check in, she asked Lilly, "Do you know his prognosis?" My wife immediately demanded, "Why did you say 'prognosis' and not 'diagnosis'?" But we knew.

Lilly met me for an appointment in palliative care, where we sat down with a woman who asked us about advanced directives and living wills. We were making plans for my fucking death. Try looking someone you love in the eyes when you know you're that sick. Try sitting with them and deciding what goes where and who gets what. I could see what Lilly was thinking—she'd been expecting thirty more years with this man, but now it might be two, and it wasn't fair.

Feeling lightheaded, I gripped the arms of the chair and sank back. I closed my eyes. No one gets more than they can handle? I've had to fight tooth and nail for everything I have. I've heard others talk about how their parents cosigned on loans or leases or how their grandma had died and left them some money. That was never me.

I turned to face Lilly. "I want you to know that I'm going to fight this. I didn't come this far, from the fucking dirt, to give up."

When I got home, I followed the path behind the house down to the river. Standing on that sandy beach, I thought, *Yes, I'm dying from cancer. But I've come so close to getting shot so many times before; I'm living my bonus days, sitting here on seven acres of my own land. Just take a look at my life, dude. I should be able to walk into this river right this second and be okay.*

"So what the hell am I so sad about?!" I cried out in desperation. But I knew why. What tore me apart was the thought of Lilly, Sabina, and my godchildren hurting because of me. I was worried about Bina, that she'd close right up and this would crush her. What if her old man died and she turned to a little bit of coke? Would something click into place and a switch flip inside her, like it had for me? The possibility of Lilly drinking again brought me to my knees. And I couldn't bear the thought of Makana and Landon calling out for Ro-Ro when they needed me…but I'd be gone.

When the news spread, there was a constant stream of family and friends who wanted to see me. I pulled out mementos from my box of memories: little Indian Head coins, my mom's ring, and my dad's jewelry box from Hong Kong, made of sterling silver. Inside that box, Dad had collected cuff ties with emerald stones from Italy, Israel, and India that he'd bought during his time in the service. After years of pawning off items for drug money, there wasn't much left. And what I did have, I wanted to leave for loved ones anyway. This was my chance to look them in the eyes and give things away so they could enjoy them now.

Once everyone left, I wiped off the dust on my photo album and randomly pulled old pictures from their sleeves, tossing them away. The doctors had confirmed I had stage IV lung cancer and it was everywhere. I didn't know if I was about to fucking die, so I was downsizing. As I sifted through the past, I found a few pieces of Sabina's artwork from when she was young—a poster declaring me the "Best dad hands down," made from her little girl handprints, a plate with Hanukkah blessings, and a paper dreidel. And so many handwritten birthday cards.

I want her to know one day when I'm gone: I didn't just throw everything away. I'd held onto these.

***

I know the coronavirus took lives, but I believe it saved mine. During the early months of the pandemic, new hospital protocols limited nonessential treatments. Beds sat empty. Within days of my diagnosis, a neurosurgeon performed an ablation procedure to freeze and destroy the tumor on my spine. Afterward, I started radiation to target all the tumors in my body. While my team was dedicated to expediting my care plan, these treatments came with their own set of side effects. The radiation to my chest led to pulmonary fibrosis, leaving my lung scarred. Today, scans show that I'm missing a third of my lung, so I'll have moments when I struggle to catch my breath.

After the final round of treatment, they wheeled me over to ring the bell in celebration. It was a Saturday morning, and with social distancing, there were just a couple of nurses and me. From my wheelchair, I grasped at the thick white rope hanging down. Gone were the days when I could lift an entire living room wall of studs by myself. The nurses had to help me tighten my fingers around the rope. I slowly moved my wrist back and forth till we finally heard a faint ding. I gave a small smile from the corner of my mouth. I was a fighter. I wasn't finished yet.

From the beginning, I made it clear to every doctor that I didn't want any opioids. I didn't want to risk taking anything addictive; I just told them I was allergic. When they suggested prescribing medical marijuana to increase my appetite, I politely declined and forced myself to eat instead, even if it was a mini cucumber every day. After surgery, when the pain became unbearable, they offered me morphine tablets. I only took a couple home and had Lilly hand them to me. A week's supply? No thanks.

As I recovered from the initial radiation treatments and my spine strengthened, my oncologist presented another treatment option called immunotherapy. It would help my body find and fight the cancer cells by boosting my immune system. Lilly and I did our own research and learned that when immunotherapy was combined with chemotherapy in clinical trials, people called it the "new miracle drug" for longer, fuller lives. In the fine print, only a small percentage of patients experienced severe reactions and had to discontinue the treatment. Signed and signed.

Lilly and I were excited when I was approved to start. I'd be around for a long time. Everything would be okay. I rode the elevator up to the tenth floor of the Mayo Clinic, and on that first visit, I saw Josephine, the wife of an AA buddy. She leaned in for a hug and whispered, "I saw the name on the chart, and I was really hoping it wasn't you." We both cried.

I visited medical oncology at least once a week, often enough to become a regular. As a guy who was once homeless, I splurged on valet parking, and the drivers got to know me by name. "Hey, Rory! We've got a space for you! Pull up here!" After the appointments, I'd make my way down with a cane, struggling step by step, clenching my teeth to hold the vomit back and clenching my ass to hold the shit in. The valets would help me climb into my truck. When I got home, I'd drag myself up the stairs and collapse into bed. I needed to face this alone; watching the people I love choke up on sight was too much for me.

I tolerated the first few treatments okay, but by the third, I started to waver. While I walked in with a group of people, I watched them leave through my window, one by one, while I remained hooked up to an IV. For six grueling hours. The result of advanced cancer. The nurses would run three pre-chemo drugs, then the chemo itself, and finally, arrange for the infusion of the immunotherapy—the "miracle drug."

I endured ten rounds of treatment, and during the winter of 2020, I found myself in the ER six times. I developed pneumonitis, where my lungs were so inflamed that oxygen couldn't pass through them. My oxygen levels were so low that if they didn't improve soon, the doctors planned to intubate me and transfer me to the ICU. They couldn't risk straining my heart. My thoughts shifted to Sabina, Lilly, Makana, and Landon, and I held on tight. Was I about to die here? I didn't know. I wasn't angry that I had cancer. It sucked, but I wasn't angry anymore. No more of the "it's not fair, and I didn't get enough time" talk. I just didn't want to fucking suffer. I feel like I've suffered enough in my life. I'd rather it go bad real quick and be done.

During the whole week I was held in the hospital, Lilly kept telling me the eagles that always hung around our place had disappeared (she'd look for them every day). But the minute I got home, they showed up and perched on a tree branch near my bedroom window, like they were keeping watch over me.

It turned out I was in the unlucky five percent of patients who couldn't tolerate immunotherapy. The doctors explained my immune system had overactivated and started attacking my healthy cells too. That treatment was off the table now; if I tried it even one more time, it would take my life. Again, my legs were knocked from under me.

I sat Lilly down next to me and gave her an out. "Maybe this would be a good time for you to check out, honey. Obviously, I won't be around for much longer. There's no reason you should stick around and watch me deteriorate and die."

She bucked up and gave it to me straight. "We've come this far together and you think I'm gonna fucking leave you? I love you, you idiot!" Whoa, let's put away anything that could be thrown.

I knew it before, but I learned again just how much she loves me.

***

When I first got sick and had to spend a night at the hospital, Lilly's mom came to visit. I could tell her parents were worried about leaving Lilly alone, especially when they heard her sobbing into the phone, sharing the news about my health. Her mom didn't know I was preparing to ask Lilly for two promises: first, to find a decent man when I'm gone; and second, to never drink again. She wants to honor me after I'm gone? I told her, that's what I want then. Her sobriety is my dying wish because I know, if she ever starts drinking vodka again, she'll drink herself to death.

We called Sabina and could sense how scared she was for me too. She came over for dinner with us one evening, but we kept the conversation light: How's your boyfriend? How's your job going? Sabina was twenty-three now, and she was on her own path of discovering what she wanted in life.

At the start of my fight with cancer, I posted on social media to let others know what was going on. After a while, I stopped sharing updates about my health. Whenever people found out, they would naturally ask, "How are you? How's it going? Keep us posted, okay?"

But cancer is like swinging on a pendulum:

My scans are looking really good!

But I can't have the immunotherapy anymore. It could kill me.

I'm doing great this week!

Yeah, I'm back in the ER; I've got pneumonitis.

I'm out now!

I'm in the ER again.

I either felt okay afterward or so sick to my stomach that I could barely walk. I didn't want to lie to people when they asked about me, but I could hear their voices choking up on the other end. After the first few rounds of treatment, I realized I was

217

dragging people down with me because their emotions depended on how Rory was doing that day. My daughter, my godkids, and the people I loved. So Lilly and I made the decision to keep things between the two of us. We've told everyone that when things are good, we'll share, and when they aren't, they can count on us to keep fighting. We agreed that if things get really bad, we'll say something. And have left it at that.

I tried googling my prognosis, and of course, the stats varied depending on the article. From what I've read, only 5 to 8 percent of people with stage IV lung cancer make it past five years. I was diagnosed in April 2020, just passing the three-year mark. I'm grateful to live just minutes away from the greatest hospital in the world, known for its cancer research. The doctors won't give any specific estimate, though. Even when I try to trick them. "So, in your experience with other patients with a similar cancer, as a whole, would you say more or less of them survive past…" They always cut me off with a chuckle, knowing what I'm after.

"Rory, listen. You're asking for my experience, but there are seven other doctors working out there with different experiences."

Every now and then, I'll have a scary episode. A few nights ago, I was sitting at the dinner table and suddenly started sweating like crazy. When I stood up, I had to hold on to the table to steady myself. They call these "cancer hot flashes." If it happens again, they'll call me in for a brain MRI (my third one) to make sure the cancer hasn't spread upward.

In 2020, I had plenty of on-the-ground-and-begging moments—moments when I questioned, "Why me?" Some days, I'd lie in it; others, I'd dust myself off with, "Because I'm a total badass." Because I have the gift of gab and I've been put on this Earth to inspire others. That's why I have cancer. Even if I were wrong, I don't give a shit; that thought was the only fucking way I could get on with my day.

There were people all around me who followed my fight and found hope for themselves or a loved one. A lady at the cleaners. A radiology tech. A girl at the Kwik Trip gas station. One morning, after treatments, I slowly plopped down on a bench near Mayo's valet service and ended up talking to a couple from Wisconsin for twenty-five minutes. We shared our stories and shed some tears. I didn't know who they were, but when the wife left, she carried more encouragement to keep holding on than she'd had when she first sat down. That's why I have cancer—for people like her.

***

There are a lot of things I can't do anymore, like getting through a day without needing to lie down, or vacuuming the house without feeling it in my back, or going for a long walk without gasping. That's why, in January 2022, I made the decision to sell my business to the foreman of my siding crew, and all of my rental properties too.

It hurt letting Rory's go. I had an emotional attachment to it, something you're never supposed to do in business. But in my heart, when I dug deep enough and sat in a quiet place, I believed it was the right thing to do. I didn't know if I had two weeks or ten years left. I still don't. So I didn't want to grind it out till the last minute and die. And with the rentals, it was tough dealing with phone calls at 9:30 on Sunday nights. "Hey, the toilet won't flush," or, "The neighbors upstairs are making too much noise." I believed that the added stress and pressure would chip away at the number of days I had left.

219

In these next couple of years, I plan to do things that may seem foolish to people on the outside. When I drove my Cadillac to the dealership to explore trade-in options, I spotted a stunning blue seventieth anniversary 2023 Corvette Stingray in the middle of the showroom. It looked just like the Lamborghini poster I had hanging over my bed when I was seven. The engine behind the seat and a trunk in the front and back. As I sat in the driver's seat, gripping the steering wheel tight, I imagined taking Lilly to a fancy dinner at Pittsburgh Blue for a night out. I thought, if I were to get sick again, I'd be mad at myself for walking away. People might say I'm showing off, but I don't care about the judgment. I can't afford to play the waiting game anymore. I drove the Corvette home that very same day. I'm determined to make as many dreams come true as I can while I still can. I'll have fun, and my wife can sell it later.

Life is the space between the starting line—when you're born—and the finish line—when the curtain falls. Indian Mike taught me this way of thinking, to visualize it, and I shared it with Eric and Steve, the fathers of my godchildren. I told them, "Take your age and place yourself on this timeline. 'X' marks the spot. How will you spend the time you've got left? What do you want your life to be?"

What if I get sick this winter? Maybe these are my last three to four months. People around me say, "Oh, you'll be fine. You look so great!" but I'm not in denial. I'm not trying to feel sorry for myself. I've just accepted that I'm a walking miracle on a timeline that's shrinking fast.

There's been a lot of pain in my life. Pain and misery can push us to change and put our feet firmly on the ground. But, for a long time, my threshold for what was considered miserable was incredibly high, given everything I've endured: begging on the streets, living in crack houses, going hungry for days. That's why I kept bouncing from one jail cell to the next for so long. But that tolerance has lessened over the years with every good moment I've had: watching Sabina in a school play, meeting Lilly, holding my godbabies. These days, if I'm not at peace with myself when I wake up, then I'll change my situation, whether that's my habits, my home, or my job.

We're so scared of the unknown. People stay married for thirty-five years when they weren't happy twenty years ago. Why? Because it's familiar. Because of the kids. Because it's just easier that way. Or maybe because we don't know whether anyone else would want us. It's the unknown, and we lack the strength, the belief in ourselves, and the understanding that we're limited on time to change our situations. It's just what we do—we keep on keeping on—and thirty years later, we sit with regrets.

When I met Lilly, she was so young, but I didn't care what others thought. I'd stare at her in church like a weirdo. She moved me. When outsiders observe us, they might assume, "He must be loaded." But no, I didn't have a dime when I met her. She worked two jobs as a waitress, and I was at Rob's Construction, living in my tiny Seventh Street house. We both felt a connection, took a chance, and tried.

With my "X" approaching the end of the line, I'm determined to keep seeking out joy. Life doesn't have to be perfect, but it's gotta be pretty damn good.

Rory with Lilly during cancer treatments

LET THE GOOD THINGS YOU DO DEFINE YOU

In jail, I'd tear maps from the *National Geographic* magazines and stick them on my wall. I'd study them, memorizing the names of the little islands in the South Pacific. Lying on my thin mattress, with my arms crossed under my head, I'd escape into a bungalow sitting over sparkling waters in the sunlight.

In 2018, Lilly and I flew to Tahiti and Bora Bora. We checked into Pearl Resorts, where we were greeted with flower garlands and ferried to our private bungalow. My wife and I looked at each other, an alcoholic and a drug addict, and I broke down crying in front of the gal who was still there showing us the room. In the mornings, we'd sip coffee and peer through the glass-bottom floor of our hut, watching the fish swim by. Then, we'd put on our snorkel gear and swim alongside the gentle stingrays.

I've traveled to the Bahamas, the Galapagos Islands, Ecuador, Eleuthera, Puerto Rico, Saint Thomas, Costa Rica, and Saint Croix. In Las Vegas, we stayed at the Bellagio and rented a Lamborghini for a day to drive across the Hoover Dam. A year later, I returned to Vegas, but this time, I took my entire staff from Rory's with me. To reach your dreams is priceless, especially for a guy who was just trying to survive the day for so long. When I was eighteen, I used to imagine surfing the infamous Soup Bowl one day and would repeat, "Barbados in February... Barbados in February..." A few years ago, when we pulled into a dirt parking lot in Barbados, most of the surfers were tan twenty-somethings with dreadlocks, their every move getting documented by videographers. We watched a guy race against a nine-foot wave; he made it a few hundred feet before the water swallowed him whole. Amazingly, he emerged on the other side, gracefully cutting back and forth as if he'd surfed that wave a million times. It made me wonder if that could have been me, if I'd never learned to make crack from cocaine. I grabbed my surfboard, paddled out, and managed to stand up a few times. I gave it my best shot, but I knew the waves were just too powerful for someone who was out of shape and out of practice. Back on shore, I joined Lilly, still proud to have surfed one of the world's greatest waves in Barbados in February.

A part of me believes that if I want to have this life, I can't just stand by and watch others struggle. It explains why I've crossed paths with so many men and women over the years. It's as if God looks down on me and says, "See this guy? We have to keep him busy. We've got to give him all the people, all the time, as many as we can. If he has even five seconds to himself, he'll be off getting high again. He's going to have to do some shit, or he'll never make it."

Once, my buddy and I were walking along downtown Rochester near the library when we saw a Jeep flip near us. I ran to the couple trapped inside, with my friend shouting behind me, "Rory! Wait! There's fuel leaking!" My legs were already in motion before I could even fully process what had happened. I kicked in the window and dragged them out. I knew I had to fucking try. I couldn't stop myself.

Just this evening, with some extra cash on me, I stopped at the

Hyvee grocery store on the way home from working at my flip house. I asked for five twenty-dollar gift cards. Sometimes, I'll find older people and say, "I know groceries can be expensive. I have these cards, but I don't need them all. Would you like one?" I've spent more time feeling bad about myself than good; so now, when something feels right inside, I latch on to it. Some say thank you and some hesitate before accepting one. But every so often, some say no before I can even finish my sentence. I felt that rejection tonight; it was too familiar. For a moment in the canned food aisle, it was like I was standing on a street corner all over again, hearing a car door lock click shut at the sight of me.

I tell my guys that people might have bad things to say about you, but that shouldn't define you. The good you do should. And this is the secret of it all: you don't tell people the good you're doing, because then it becomes about you. Just knowing you did it—or at least knowing you tried—is enough. So, when I do die, I hope it's while I'm helping someone, not from fucking cancer.

These days, I have CT scans every three months. They've been showing what they call "no evidence of disease." But, on the last one, they found a six-millimeter spot on my left lung. If it grows any more, they'll hit it with radiation. For now, the doctors aren't too concerned. They don't have the science to explain why I'm doing so well without immunotherapy. Maybe enough of the drug got in and did its work before they had to cut it off. Maybe I don't need to know why. Maybe I just live.

Still, I was grateful for the chance to say thank you when Lilly and I received an invitation to the Eagles Cancer Telethon. From a reserved table, we listened to a team of doctors from the Mayo Clinic speak about the importance of funding cancer research. The Hormel Institute, a cancer research center, also had a group of medical researchers present. Their director spoke to the crowd of three hundred. I was shocked when I was introduced to speak next. I wasn't prepared, but then again, I never am.

I walked up to the microphone, nervous for about a minute and thirty seconds as I talked about my diagnosis. And then it hit me. I knew exactly what the researchers in the room needed to hear. "Yes, I did the chemo and radiation. But I believe the reason I'm here today is because of the immunotherapy drugs." Then I sat on the edge of the stage, climbed off, and walked to an empty chair near the Hormel group. I sat eye-to-eye with them and said, "I want you to know that all those fucking hours you spend with your little eye in a microscope doing what you do, people thinking you're weird, is why I'm here. I'm telling you that what you do is the only fucking reason I'm alive today. And I'm so grateful for that." It came from the heart, and afterward, people found me to share their own stories of cancer. I was touched to gain their trust.

It's a goal of mine to make a large monetary gift to the Mayo Clinic over the next few years. I've made an official commitment to Mayo's Department of Development, and every year, they invite Lilly and me out for coffee. I was once trying to raise twelve more dollars for a single fucking rock, and now to be able to make thousand-dollar donations?

I wish my mom were alive to see this. Me and Lilly at the same building she and I walked through for her medical appointment when I was young. The same building I'd gaze up at from the Pathway House. From being called an asshole and a piece of shit in my life to holding a letter from the Mayo Clinic calling me a *philanthropist*, thanking me for my *philanthropy*. Lilly made me get rid of that letter when she got tired of hearing me read it over and over: "You're not even saying the word right!"

RORY'S LETTER TO
THE PERSON STRUGGLING
WITH ADDICTION

Dear Friend,

We're fighting a disease here. We're not weak. No one knows why some people have it. Something inside us clicks when we drink and fires up the pleasure we get from it. It's not inside everyone, but it is inside us. A switch that flips where one drink becomes two, two become four…till we need it every day.

People on the outside might say, "Just quit already and go to treatment." They don't understand your body can't function without the effects of the drug anymore. That it's like fighting the urge to drink water. That you need it to feel normal. That it hijacks your judgment and impulse control. It's not personal. No one chooses to become obsessed with alcohol. It's brain chemistry, and the same thoughts consume you: Where's the bottle? How much do I have left? Are they asleep yet? When can I have my drink? I need a drink. I wish they'd just fucking go to bed. You make little shitty comments because you're just waiting.

Finally, you grab the ice cubes and drop them in the glass. The sound of that. You can taste it. Cracking the Bacardi. Smelling it.

Tipping the cup toward your lips. Habitual motions. The fucking obsession. Alters your mood and how you treat the people you love for a fucking drink. That's why it destroys people, lives, and families. Not everybody, though. Some can say, "Oh, I'll just have half a glass. I've got work tomorrow." But not you or me. We don't have that ability.

But buddy, you're going to have to do something different. Or you're going to be sitting here all by yourself in your nice pretty house with your fucking drink. I mean, if that's what you want, keep it up and that's what you're going to get. Not just at night when everyone's in bed. But all fucking day long. And you can sit and promise, "It's the last one," or, "Only on Fridays," or, "It'll never happen again," or, "I didn't mean what I said." All these broken, bottomless promises. If your partner is actually strong enough (not weak enough, let's get that straight) to tolerate that for so long, it's only going to become worse. Eventually, it'll implode, and all the while, there are the children seeing this over a drink. Over liquid in a cup that alters and controls you. How your mood is going to go, how much you'll get done, how you're going to treat them. The quality of life you're going to have. All determined by what you're pouring into a cup.

You can say, "I don't have a choice," but I say, "Yeah, we do." Before that first drink, when we're still sober, we have a choice to pick it up. We have a choice to go and buy a bottle of Bacardi Rum and a liter of cola. But once we start, we don't have a fucking choice anymore. We lose that choice by how it affects our mind, body, and spirit. You see, once it's in us, we drink because we have to. It's not about having fun anymore.

But you can't change something that doesn't exist. You've got to be honest with yourself and put everything on the table. If you can admit you've got a problem and own up to all the damage it's been causing, then you can start doing something about it. Turn things around.

There will be moments when it will get hard, and that's why you'll have someone else in your life to help you. Someone like me. Who won't turn their back on you. Who will be there. No matter what. And even if you fuck up again, they'll still be there. They'll never leave your fucking side. Them and whatever your higher power is, if you've got one. Together, you'll fucking do this. You don't have to do it alone.

We both know what our habit is going to give us. It's going to give us exactly what we need, and that's what makes it so perfect. So now, it's about finding the strength so we don't turn to our habit. Maybe that means new routines in your life that don't put you back in that situation where it's 9:00 p.m. and you're reaching for whatever it is that's going to fill you up. Maybe 9:00 p.m. becomes your new workout time. But before any of that can happen, you've got to give the tiniest bit of acknowledgment that all your waiting and wanting and thinking and obsessing over your habit maybe isn't normal.

It won't be a straight line, and you'll have to toughen up. If your friend goes to the ER for diabetes shock, he'll get compassion. But if you relapse, you'll likely get blame and shame. If you sit in that, you might never get back up. So dust yourself off and keep walking. His body takes in sugar differently, just like your body takes in alcohol differently. Neither is in our control. And we can never fully will it away. After all these years of being sober, I'm still not willing to chance it now. I don't want to lose what I have today. But if things get bad enough and I stop caring about what I have in life, I know I could use again. I know that. I'm conscious enough. This isn't something you master. It's always lurking. I know where the closest liquor store is and that it'll take me twelve minutes to get there. In twelve minutes, I could have an ice-cold Bacardi in that cup. What normal fucking person could even say that to another person? That I'll feel it and taste it going down my throat in twelve minutes.

You've got to remember, this is a disease. Not a moral failing. But it's a disease that we can manage. Ours is a chronic, treatable, condition. You're not alone. Most of us have some habit that we're fearful is an addiction or is slowly becoming one. Alcohol, nicotine, marijuana, and painkillers are common ones. But maybe we're finding we're on our phones too much or always quick to reach for something sweet. Maybe it's our daily need for a jolt of caffeine in the morning, or one-click shopping on Amazon, or buying that roll of lottery tickets. How we feed off the reward of seeing a comment on our post, or that taste of milk chocolate. Maybe our habit is helping us numb feelings that are too hard to face at first, but with time, it might become something we have *to do. And if we own up to just how much it's impacting our lives, this question is one for all of us:*

What will we choose while it's still a choice?

AFTERWORD

When I began my weekly interviews with Rory in the fall of 2021, I was drowning in the challenges of an ALC teacher's life: Giving instructions while some students were on their phones and others rolled in late. Students claiming they were tired during work time and would just do the assignment tomorrow. One student asking to use the bathroom and returning twenty-five minutes later. If I pushed too hard, they might shut down or stop coming altogether, and I couldn't help an absent student.

I was walking on eggshells around everyone's needs, often feeling disappointed to be working harder than the students. I questioned what many teachers do multiple times a year, sometimes even in a single school day: was I making any difference at all? That's when a student yelled out, "Shut up, bitch!"

I shared the latest hit with Rory. His response sunk deep:

Well, no shit. Wow? What do you want me to say? That's Nathan. He's teaching more patience than any other student. If we give up on them this quick, where else will these kids go? And Nathan may never make it. He may not change, but as the adults, we have to be able to look each other in the eye and say we tried—really tried. He's a kid who needs us to love him the most. That doesn't mean pointing out his defects and everything he did wrong this week.

If Rory's anything, it's direct. As I met with him to learn his story, I didn't know just how much of a mentor he'd become to me. I took his messages to heart and brought them into the classroom with me.

Over the next week, I knew I wasn't welcome in Nathan's space. Head down. Sitting in the back. No comment when asked to join in the day's activity. But I had to be able to look myself in the eye. I handed Nathan a note, apologizing for imposing a plan for extra tutoring without hearing his thoughts first and for discussing it in the middle of a crowded hallway. I said his words had cut deep and that I needed to hear an apology in return, and hoped he would stay after class so we could talk through his ideas to help him do well. I think the care I showed him earlier in the year when I had remembered his birthday and we celebrated in class helped here, because the next day, Nathan stayed.

Over the following months, we built a study hall into his schedule and involved his family in providing extra support at home. Since his dad was in jail and his mom was absent, his uncle stepped up. When I first met Nathan, he had a permanent smirk of defiance, but by the third quarter, he was passing most of his classes.

So, when I learned that Nathan had shoved a student in class, that resulted in stitches, I was devastated for all involved. He would be transferred to online school for the remainder of the year. As I watched him process the news, withdrawn, I knew what a blow this was. The next day, I stopped by the computer lab and found him sitting with his head down. I quietly told him, "I'm proud of you for showing up today."

We were on different schedules now, so I didn't see him again after that. When the school year was drawing to a close, I was surprised to see Nathan making his way to an empty chair by my desk. When he didn't say anything, I asked how things were going. He answered my questions politely, using the fewest words possible. Then, he stood, his thumbs hooked around his backpack straps, and softly said, "Okay, bye then," before walking out. That was the sum of my interactions with Nathan: he had found a safe place to rest for a moment and recharge. I wonder, with guilt, without Rory's voice in my ear, how would I have treated Nathan, and where would he be now?

Since I spent five days a week in the classroom, I often listened to Rory's memories on our Saturday morning chats with my students in mind. I itched for the insights he'd learned in sponsoring over a hundred men, many of them "hard cases." Each time, I left with the messages I needed to hear the most.

A couple of months into the school year, three girls dragged chairs into the hallway to talk. I asked them to please go to their classes. Sophia pointed to her friend and said, "She needs us. There's no other place to go."

"Listen, you guys really can't be in the hallway right now. How about you come into my classroom, instead?"

"But you've got a class in there. We don't want everyone listening."

"Well, it isn't a choice to stay in the hallway. It sends the wrong message. Just sit in the back of my room and talk things out. Everyone's busy doing their work."

The other two shifted in their seats away from me with their arms crossed. Sophia firmly said, "We're not moving."

"And, as I said, that's not a choice." I could feel my blood pressure rising as her tone grew sharper and more defiant. We all stood our ground, waiting for the other to give in. In the end, the girls slam-stuffed their backpacks and stormed off.

The best way to communicate with anyone in this world is by staying level. Instead of saying, "These kids…" or, "Those students…" how about we say "Mary" and "Jack" and see them as human beings? The way we word things creates power dynamics, but we've got to check ourselves: They're not less than us. Because that's what blocks the connection.

From the moment I spotted the girls through my classroom window, I didn't really see Sophia, Tanya, and Hailey. I saw "those kids" who were always in the hallways. I believed I was listening to their needs and offering choices, being fair and empathetic—the ALC way. But I'd stood over them and created those choices from *all the way up here* for these girls who were *all the way down there.* It was never really a "we" conversation. I stepped off the pedestal and wrote individual notes:

Sophia,

There are things I wish I had done differently yesterday afternoon. It says a lot about you that you wanted to be there for your friend when she was upset. I should have acknowledged that first, instead of jumping to frustration about you being in the hallway. I could feel my blood pressure rising and yours too. That wasn't helpful for either of us. We could have agreed to a reasonable time limit for you to finish your conversation and then head to class.

I was angry and didn't consider how you tend to be a leader at our school. In all of our past encounters, I've seen how you speak kindly and politely, even when those around you don't. Had I remembered, I would have known that if you were fighting me this hard, your friend must have really needed you. Keep acting by your values.

A few days later, I found the following note in my mailbox:[3]

Mrs. Patel,

I'm sorry for making you feel disrespected by the way I was talking to you. I've been working on my reactions, but sometimes it's really hard. You were just trying to get us where we were supposed to be and we made it harder than it needed to be.

Again, thank you for taking the time to write us these. It means a lot to know you care and even more of a thank-you for everything you said at the end.

❤ *Sophia*

Her note sparked a light in my teacher's heart again, and I consciously checked myself now: Was I seeing behaviors, or was I seeing human beings? Was I talking *with* students or *at* them?

Around the same time, I absorbed a colleague's advisory students. On our first day together, I announced that we'd be playing a series of get-to-know-you games throughout the week and shared directions for that day's activity. There was Nathan, chuckling with his friends in the back. His posture read, "Sure, I'll do it, but I'm not going to like it." Mario and Savannah, who loved games, were already writing. Then there were Maya and Paige, with their arms crossed.

"Do you guys need something to write with?" I asked.

Maya answered, "No. I'm not doing this."

"Same," Paige echoed.

If you're not able to connect emotionally with someone, no matter what you say or how you say it, it's not going to resonate. To get past

---

[3] Reprinted with permission. Names have been changed.

their emotional walls from years of hearing people talk at them, I start out with something positive. That might lift the curtain just enough that I can get in. Not some fake shit like, "That's a nice shirt." Instead, say something like, "The last two days, you've shown up to school on time. That's awesome." Do your research, because they'll catch you in a fib. Or you could go for a laugh and add, "You sure you're feeling okay?" You see, the connection starts with the smile he gives you. That means, the next time you say something, he's going to stop and listen.

I made a point to compliment Maya and Paige on their fashion nails and their bedazzled purses, things that were important to them. I watched them console a friend and praised them after. When I checked in with them about an assignment, they declined any help, but this time it was polite. During an extended advisory day, I set up cooking stations for "no-bake desserts," and smiled as I watched the group bond through the challenge. I played some music in the background, and we all laughed at my playlist of slow, melancholy songs. "No, I'm not going through a terrible breakup! I just like this song!"

The next day, when it was time for grade checks, students took turns reviewing their progress with me. When I called Maya's name, she walked over and I did a little dance in my head. I started with, "I was a little nervous about trying those cookies you made yesterday. Would I live another day?" She was grinning.

Once you're in, try to encourage them, but don't make it too obvious. Kids aren't stupid. You can't jump to, "Oh, we're so proud of you!" Easy, easy. Some of these kids have never been told something nice. They've only heard "You're no good," or, "You'll never be nothing." You have no idea what goes on in their house, and for some, it's really ugly.

"Maya, you've got two As, two Bs, and a C here. Look at your grades from last year, and then this quarter's. That's a huge improvement."

When you've got him for a second, he can go in a heartbeat. Then you'll have to look for another moment, another chance, to get in around that curtain. So, go!

"Let's talk about your last period. I see an F here. Can you tell me about that class? What's going on?" Before, her reply would have been a passive shoulder shrug or a more direct, "Nothing's going on. Can I go?" But now, I got to hear her side of the story.

When some people first hear that I work at the ALC, I get a look of sympathy. "It must be so hard with those kids. Good for you." I want to respond by slamming my plate of food down and ranting, "Listen here! Every day, I get to be inspired because they're some of the most resilient people I've ever met." During one of our talks, when Rory shared about how he consciously shows the men he works with all of the mountains they've already climbed, it struck a chord. All of the years of missed opportunities hit me, but I was determined to help students recognize their own strength now.

I've had hundreds of conversations with people battling addictions where I reflect the truth of their journey and hope that a little bit of light shines through. I say, "You were up all night, doing what you needed to do to survive, finding places to sleep, and scrounging up enough change for a meal. You just need someone like me to look you in the eye and tell you that you have all the ability in the world. You've already shown it. In our addiction, we've shown it. Let's incorporate it into something good now."

In the middle of the school year, during an independent English project, Amanda was crafting a personal narrative about her Xanax addiction—how it started, how bad it got, and her road to recovery. I used our precious one-on-one feedback time intentionally: "So, you're saying when you decided to quit, you left all your friends behind? That must have taken a lot of courage to start over sober," and, "I'm surprised your coworkers are bringing pills into work. But you've been saying no. That takes strength." Later, when she expressed fears of failure while considering a nursing assistant program after graduation, I used parts of her essay to remind her: "You were involved in two car accidents on the same day because of those pills. You were skipping school, smoking weed, getting high, failing classes. And now, here you are, getting ready to walk across the stage and receive your diploma. You've already proven how much you can do. So go out there and see what happens."

While Amanda was writing, Jessica was drafting a presentation about toxic relationships. She merged research with her own experience and wrote, "He would tear me apart, and to cope, I self-harmed, smoked weed, and drank. When I finally let him go, I had to learn how to stand on my own. I still have shoulder issues from the dislocations, scars, and scrapes, but I get up every day. I eat. I shower. I take care of my pets. I come to school. I'm not staying down."[4] I made it a point to help Jessica acknowledge her own resilience, too. I wanted both of these girls to remember the mountains they've already climbed the next time they faced a challenge. You *can. I'll show you.*

Both students agreed to give an optional presentation to a freshman class and dedicated hours to seeking feedback, revising their work, and practicing their delivery. It reminded me that

---

[4] Reprinted with permission.

when students have a personal interest in their work and a real audience to share it with, magic happens. Amanda and Jessica spoke about addictions and toxic relationships to a room full of people. They invited their moms too. I hope they experienced what Rory does when he speaks to a crowd: the reassurance that what they endured could be a source of hope for others.

I confided in Rory that every single day, I have at least one student (on harder days, one in each period) who rests their head on the table, eyes open but blank. A kid who's going through something tough right then. It might be big, maybe small. Might be something they have control over, or maybe not. Lots of maybes till I can get them to open up and share.

You know, teachers might say, "I care about my students. I'm always asking how they're doing." But you shouldn't even be asking that. You just have to look at their eyes to know they're not doing well. How they've been wearing the same clothes for three days. People have to understand it from our side, how it makes us feel like shit. If you want to do something nice, then give a fucking smile. And stop asking, "What are your plans this weekend?" Uh, let my dad fucking beat on me and not eat for two days? You're bringing the weekend that hasn't even happened yet into the conversation and ruining his day.

Sometimes, you've got to show them that you know them and that you care without you saying it. A lot of them don't want to hear nothing; all they hear at home is all kinds of shit. Maybe then, you've got a chance they'll open up. But if you're stuck and all you got are words, just make statements: "If I can help, I will," or a simple, "It's good to see you today, John." If you show the students you're here, they'll come a little earlier to your class or stay a little later. When someone finds a spot, they're there.

When Maria was gone for a string of days, I asked her to walk a few laps with me around the school so we could talk. I told her I'd been worried and had missed her. She shared that her mom had swallowed a bunch of pills and she had to help her vomit them out. Maria had been staying home to make sure her mom wouldn't try it again. She finally got to come to school today because her older sister was back, and it was a relief to be here. I showed her the social worker's office, a resource she could use when she was ready. Later, when I saw her in there, it was a heavy weight to know that Maria only got the help she needed because she had confided in me. And she only confided in me because I'd shown her I cared. A teacher's work.

Not long after, Rory visited the ALC to speak to my class. The following Saturday, his words hit home:

I read one of your student's letters, how her parents verbally abuse her day in and day out when they're drunk. I fear for her because, at her age, she can already handle shit to another level. She might go through life, working a shitty job, in a shitty relationship, and think, "Oh, it's not that bad," because she grew up seeing worse. Meanwhile, an outsider looking in would say, "Are you fucking kidding? That's horrible!" But for her to see it that way, it's got to be extreme. That's the scary part.

What she doesn't know is that what she grew up seeing was fucking hell. She didn't get to go live with grandparents with meatloaf for dinner and a couple of presents under the tree. Where it's eleven o'clock on a Friday night and there's no screaming, no stench of vodka or Bacardi or tequila. No bottles getting smashed. Even though she saw it for nineteen years, it's NOT okay. Neither is the way her boss and boyfriend are treating her now. It's not just "kinda bad." Hopefully, with what you guys do at the ALC, you can break that cycle and give them opportunities to see what life and people can be.

It was spring semester, and Rory's message for the ALC bolstered my passion for helping to organize our student-centered Wednesdays. Once a week, we experimented with weaving extracurricular activities into the school day. The staff would dream up experiences to provide students, sometimes partnering with community organizations: Students could mentor a local elementary school student. Play multiplayer board games with classmates. Visit the local nature center for hiking, cross-country skiing, and snowshoeing. Create a step-by-step canvas painting. Volunteer at Channel One, our local food bank. Practice the art of spoken word poetry. Build set pieces for a community dance production. Create a design to be modeled in the school fashion show. Produce and record their own music.

Some may argue that activities like playing board games don't belong in the school day. But many of our students have never played a board game at home with family and friends—so when will they get the chance otherwise? *People can get caught up in their own little world, confined by all these secrets about how they've lived that they don't want anyone to know. Just being able to loosen up and be yourself—and find yourself—can help so much.* During a game of Telestrations, students and I sat around a coffee table, doubled over with laughter, without a single cell phone in sight. It was a moment when these students were a part of a healthy social experience. Isn't that exactly what school should provide? Isn't that part of my role as a teacher?

When addicts tell me "they don't got no dreams," I tell them dreams come about just living life, going places, watching TV, reading a book, maybe learning about an individual. You'll see someone or something one day, and bam! It'll inspire you. You have dreams; you just don't know it yet. Or you stay closed off to it, thinking, "I won't, I can't, this won't, my family, my upbringing..." That's the "poor me" outlook.

The more you see of the world, the more you'll allow yourself to believe. Then, later I can tell them, you have this dream for yourself now, but if you keep on the same path, you'll never get there. You don't have to be perfect. You don't have to fucking change everything. Just pick one thing that'll get you closer to the life you want, and at least try.

Maybe through our student-centered experiences, students will discover new strengths, skills, and passions they can carry with them past graduation. Maybe they can open new doors. And if Rory is right, some might even catch hold of a dream that gets them coming to school every day and trying.

After months of interviews with Rory, I looked at my pile of shorthand notes and video files and decided to apply for a sabbatical leave. That school year, I had connected with students on a deeper level than I had in my previous fourteen years at the ALC. I knew there was something special in Rory's story. Yes, there was a message for the student who felt lost and often hopeless, but there was also a message for teachers too: how to connect with those students.

During the first few months of my leave, I worked on transcribing past interviews while continuing to meet with Rory to fill in the gaps. I listened as he shared stories about Tyler, who he'd found sleeping behind his business, and how he intentionally walked side by side with him. About the time he first met a woman named Kate, who sat in a wheelchair, and asked her, "What are you staring at?" and watched her grin. *People have said there's something about me, sometimes strong, sometimes not; it comes and goes. A drive to live and enjoy life that glows from within. If it's caught at the right time, at just the right angle on the right day, it does something to people. A little of my light shines through and directly into them. I can embrace everyone I meet. From all the shit came something beautiful.*

With Rory's voice resonating in my ear more and more, a bit of that light shined through me and I started offering more smiles, nods, hellos, and good mornings. This small change gradually spread outward, transforming my conversations into genuine and meaningful encounters. I met with Nora, a local seamstress, when I had a pile of Indian outfits my ten-year-old no longer fit into. While my daughter was in the fitting room, I noticed Nora seemed a bit down as she worked on altering another client's dress. I told her how I appreciated having her in town because she worked so well with resizing Indian clothes while preserving the original design.

Nora glanced up and confided, "I've been feeling tired lately. I can't keep up like I used to."

"I'm sure it's hard working over a sewing machine all day. Strains your eyes and back."

"It's not that. My husband had a heart attack."

"What?! Nora, I'm so sorry. When did it happen?"

She had found him lying on the kitchen floor two weeks ago. At the hospital, they connected him to a machine. Her husband had just decided to temporarily stop their health insurance to pay off their house first. He was banking on Medicare starting up in a few months anyway. Nora had to make the hard choice of bringing him home. She and her teenage son took turns caring for him, but he passed away a few days later.

"I've lost so much weight because I don't feel like eating…and I don't feel like living. My son tells me to focus on him, that he's still here. I make a little money from sewing. I'll keep working as long as I can see okay."

I told her, "I know you got up this morning, made a little breakfast for both of you, and you've been working down here since. You're doing all you can right now. You and your son will handle things together as you go. You have to believe that."

She remembered her husband. She talked, and I listened, and we both cried.

Over the next few days, my husband and I doubled the quantity of dinners we cooked and took turns dropping off food to Nora and her son. I wrote a post advertising her sewing services and shared it on a popular Rochester Facebook group page. I also sent her links to county assistance organizations and programs. Now, every few months, I send her messages to let her know I'm thinking about her. In her last reply, she wrote, "Still hurts. I'm thinking about our beautiful memories to make my days okay."

I wonder how many connections like this I missed out on before meeting Rory. How many times did I avoid initiating a conversation because I was unsure of myself or didn't think it was my place? How many times did I prematurely end a difficult conversation with a simple "I'm so sorry to hear that," without even attempting to learn more about someone's life? How many times did I miss the chance to help because I didn't take the time to learn what they needed?

I practiced staying level in conversations and breathing through the discomfort, and almost magically, the person on the other side began mirroring my openness, honesty, and vulnerability. When a friend shared about her marital conflicts, I arranged for my husband and me to meet with both of them, offering a neutral listening space. We took in their anger and resentments, shared our perspectives when appropriate, and shed light on instances of miscommunication. I reminded them of the challenges they had already overcome and how strong they were.

Both independently reached out afterward. He emailed the next morning: "Some part of me feels that sharing such details with anybody will be embarrassing, irrelevant to others, or I will be judged incorrectly. But after you guys left, I felt lighter and relieved. As if a huge burden was off my shoulders just by talking to someone about it. I cannot thank you both enough for your help, love, trust, and care."[5] Maybe he was seeing that "he" was part of a "we."

A week later, she messaged: "I can't thank you enough for coming over that day and helping us figure things out. You gave some great suggestions that I still think about and try to use. I am grateful to have a friend like you."[6]

I don't believe it's a coincidence that around the same time, two of my other friends messaged similar sentiments.

"Thank you so much. I feel fortunate to have a friend like you."

"Sweta, you're a great friend."

Both of them texted me after getting together and sharing, our walls down and our hearts open. Not filtered by what we should say, or what's appropriate to share, or how our sharing may make us look. We talked about our worries—with our children, our marriages, and our work. We asked questions to understand and then looked at the issue from the other side. Sometimes we received closure; other times, the peace that comes from simply sharing. These were genuine connections. Their random messages affirmed the strong bond they had felt in that moment too.

With each encounter where I let my guard down and felt the magic of a genuine connection, the more I wanted to practice this

---

[5] Reprinted with permission.

[6] Reprinted with permission.

skill. When I accompanied my husband to a medical appointment, I was amazed by his doctor's skillful explanation of complex medical terms in simple language. Her effort reassured us. I took a moment to let her know. In the past, I would have offered a simple thank-you and said goodbye. A missed opportunity. And when my kids' tennis coach messaged to express a late thank-you for a holiday gift, she explained her belated note: she'd been working on a thesis. I could have replied, "You're welcome, and no worries!" but instead, I took a moment to ask her about the driving question behind her thesis. This led her to share that her former tennis coach, who was like a second father to her, had recently taken his own life. She struggled to find herself on the court again and couldn't accept his decision. She was writing her paper in his honor. I had lost a good friend to suicide too, and I wrote back remembering that loss, letting my own walls down. Here were two people actively listening, freely sharing, understanding, comforting, and connecting. Rory always says this is the good stuff in life.

Each moment lifted me a little more, and a little more, till I stood erect with the trust and faith they had in me. These were the greatest moments in my life, and each one saved me. With my head down, they would have passed me by.

The braver I become, the more open I am to saying yes to experiences outside of my comfort zone. I said yes to Lilly's Ladies Supper Club invitation, even though I was immediately anxious about mingling in a room full of strangers. I said yes to playing in a women's doubles pickleball tournament—me, who for the longest time didn't trust herself to hold a ball without dropping it. And I said yes to teaching fellow gym members at Burn Boot Camp how to play the game. When two close friends separately confided that they didn't know who they were outside of being a mother and a wife and were feeling down about themselves, I invited them to join our pickleball group too. I caught a glimpse of why Rory was so dedicated to organizing events. Seeing the smiles and growth from one gathering to the next, especially in confidence, was priceless to me. These moments gave all of us an opportunity to get out of our own heads, to breathe, reset, and be *a part of.*

While working on this book, I discovered that only 2 percent of people who set out to write one actually complete it. I had many restless nights: just who did I think I was to take on this project? Just when I needed encouragement most, I bumped into two students from my early years of teaching at the ALC. We only had a few minutes to talk, but one opened up about her heroin and meth addiction and how she wanted to give treatment another try. We were standing in the middle of the public library, and she whispered to me how exhausted she was from nearly dying multiple times and desperate for something different. I met the second student while picking up my kids from school. It took a moment to adjust to his "yes, ma'am's," before he shared his own battle with meth addiction and how he had recently completed treatment. I told him I was proud of him.

Sometimes, we tell ourselves the stories we need to hear to keep going. I had to finish this book for these two former students. More so, I couldn't shake how quickly they had opened up their hearts to me after so many years. Maybe it was how I approached the conversation with empathy and a new understanding of addiction—how it's a switch that can flip inside any one of us, and when it does, just how difficult it is to break free. Or maybe it was the way I had learned to carry myself now—standing tall, my head held high, my walls down, and a smile…welcoming, curious, and authentic. (The more I practice these conscious choices, the less I'll second-guess myself and, one day I hope, just *be*.) Whatever the reason, interacting with those students solidified an answer to an even bigger question that had been weighing on me since the beginning: am I making a difference? I've come to believe the answer lies in our attempts to connect with others and be invited into their lives, behind the curtain. *I think it's beautiful what you do out at the ALC. It's not something you can learn from a textbook, to use your ability and skills to work with each individual student.*

With my sabbatical leave nearing its end, I talked with a colleague about my anxiety over returning to the classroom in the fall: what if I still felt lost? The very next afternoon, I received a message from another former student: "Looking back, you really did give a fuck about what happened to all of us, and that's not something you see every day." What she remembered most about our time together in the classroom was how she had felt cared for. When I feel lost, I'll latch on to this.

APPENDIX A

THE TWELVE STEPS OF ALCOHOLICS ANONYMOUS

1. We admitted we were powerless over alcohol—that our lives had become unmanageable.

2. Came to believe that a Power greater than ourselves could restore us to sanity.

3. Made a decision to turn our will and our lives over to the care of God as we understood Him.

4. Made a searching and fearless moral inventory of ourselves.

5. Admitted to God, to ourselves, and to another human being the exact nature of our wrongs.

6. Were entirely ready to have God remove all these defects of character.

7. Humbly asked Him to remove our shortcomings.

8. Made a list of all persons we had harmed, and became willing to make amends to them all.

9. Made direct amends to such people wherever possible, except when to do so would injure them or others.

10. Continued to take personal inventory and when we were wrong promptly admitted it.

11. Sought through prayer and meditation to improve our conscious contact with God as we understood Him, praying only for knowledge of His will for us and the power to carry that out.

12. Having had a spiritual awakening as the result of these Steps, we tried to carry this message to alcoholics, and to practice these principles in all our affairs.

APPENDIX B

BOOK CLUB DISCUSSION QUESTIONS

1. What contributed most toward Rory's addiction?

2. What contributed most toward Rory's recovery?

3. What was a turning point for Rory in his life? How so?

4. How would you describe Rory to a friend?

5. What theme stands out to you?

6. Which moment brought up a strong emotion?
   What insights did you gain?

7. Did the book change an opinion you held? If so, what?

8. Which lesson did you connect most with? Why?

9. What insights did you gain about your personal life (past or present) as a result of this book?

10. Why did the author choose to tell this story?

APPENDIX C

CHAPTER-BY-CHAPTER REFLECTION QUESTIONS

"FALLING IN LOVE," "STUCK LIKE CHUCK," "LIFE ON REPEAT," AND *"FORK IN THE ROAD"* (pages 17-69)

- Read the section below titled "Substance Use Disorder, Defined." Then, mark the items that you believe are true for Rory in the first list (Mayo Clinic's list of biological, environmental, and life experiences that can lead to addiction).

  ✓ How does Rory become addicted to drugs?

  ✓ Why does Rory struggle to control his addiction?

- Is there a habit in your life that feels like an addiction and negatively impacts your life?

✓ What biological, environmental, and other life experiences may be influencing your habit?

✓ How does your habit affect your self-perception?

✓ How does viewing addiction as a brain disorder impact your understanding of your habit?

✓ Replace "drug" with your habit in the second list (Mayo Clinic's list of drug addiction symptoms or behaviors) and mark the items that you believe apply to you. What insights does it give you?

SUBSTANCE USE DISORDER, DEFINED:
According to the Mayo Clinic, "Drug addiction, also called substance use disorder, is a disease that affects a person's brain and behavior and leads to an inability to control the use of a legal or illegal drug or medicine. Substances such as alcohol, marijuana and nicotine also are considered drugs."[7]

Face It TOGETHER, a peer-based nonprofit focused on data, science, and getting people well from addiction, states:

Continued use leads to profound changes in the brain that hijack the natural "reward pathway" of the brain. In nature, rewards usually only come with effort and after a delay. But addictive substances shortcut this process and flood the brain with chemicals that signal pleasure.

[7] Mayo Clinic Staff (2022, October 4). *Drug addiction (substance use disorder)*. Mayo Clinic. Retrieved February 26, 2023, from https://www.mayoclinic.org/diseases-conditions/drug-addiction/symptoms-causes/syc-20365112 (Used with permission of Mayo Foundation for Medical Education and Research, all rights reserved.)

When addiction takes hold, these changes in the brain erode a person's self-control and ability to make good decisions, while sending highly intense impulses to take drugs. These are the same circuits linked to survival, driving powerful urges no different from those driving the need to eat or drink water. These overwhelming impulses help explain the compulsive and often baffling behavior around addiction. People will keep using even when terrible things happen to them... Addiction is a chronic disease, which means it's a long-lasting condition that can be controlled but not cured.[8]

The Mayo Clinic adds that certain biological, environmental, and life experience factors can affect the likelihood and speed of developing an addiction[9]:

☐ **Environment.** Environmental factors, including your family's beliefs and attitudes and exposure to a peer group that encourages drug use, seem to play a role in initial drug use.

☐ **Family history of addiction.** Drug addiction is more common in some families and likely involves an increased risk based on genes. If you have a blood relative, such as a parent or sibling, with alcohol or drug addiction, you're at greater risk of developing a drug addiction.

---

[8] Common myths about addiction. Face It TOGETHER (n.d.). Retrieved February 26, 2023, from https://www.wefaceittogether.org/learn/common-myths

[9] Mayo Clinic Staff (2022, October 4). *Drug addiction (substance use disorder).* Mayo Clinic. Retrieved February 26, 2023, from https://www.mayoclinic.org/diseases-conditions/drug-addiction/symptoms-causes/syc-20365112. (Used with permission of Mayo Foundation for Medical Education and Research, all rights reserved.)

☐ **Mental health disorder.** If you have a mental health disorder such as depression, attention deficit hyperactivity disorder (ADHD) or post-traumatic stress disorder, you're more likely to become addicted to drugs. Using drugs can become a way of coping with painful feelings, such as anxiety, depression, and loneliness, and can make these problems even worse.

☐ **Peer pressure.** Peer pressure is a strong factor in starting to use and misuse drugs, particularly for young people.

☐ **Lack of family involvement.** Difficult family situations or lack of a bond with your parents or siblings may increase the risk of addiction, as can a lack of parental supervision.

☐ **Early use.** Using drugs at an early age can cause changes in the developing brain and increase the likelihood of progressing to drug addiction.

☐ **Taking a highly addictive drug.** Some drugs, such as stimulants, cocaine, or opioid painkillers, may result in faster development of addiction than other drugs. Smoking or injecting drugs can increase the potential for addiction. Taking drugs considered less addicting—so-called "light drugs"—can start you on a pathway of drug use and addiction.

Drug addiction symptoms or behaviors include, among others:

☐ Feeling that you have to use the drug regularly—daily or even several times a day

☐ Having intense urges for the drug that block out any other thoughts

☐ Over time, needing more of the drug to get the same effect

☐ Taking larger amounts of the drug over a longer period of time than you intended

☐ Making certain that you maintain a supply of the drug

☐ Spending money on the drug, even though you can't afford it

☐ Not meeting obligations and work responsibilities, or cutting back on social or recreational activities because of drug use

☐ Continuing to use the drug, even though you know it's causing problems in your life or causing you physical or psychological harm

☐ Doing things to get the drug that you normally wouldn't do, such as stealing

☐ Driving or doing other risky activities when you're under the influence of the drug

☐ Spending a good deal of time getting the drug, using the drug or recovering from the effects of the drug

☐ Failing in your attempts to stop using the drug

☐ Experiencing withdrawal symptoms when you attempt to stop taking the drug

"THE PERSON WHO NEEDS IT MOST, WE HAVE TO LOVE THE HARDEST" (pages 71-83)

- How do Rory's past interactions with others while in jail and later on the streets influence his perspective and choices?

- *The person who needs it most, we have to love the hardest.* Think of a person in your life where this phrase could be applied. How would this perspective change your behavior toward them?

***

"IF YOU WEREN'T THINKING ABOUT YOURSELF SO MUCH, MAYBE THINGS WOULDN'T BE SO BAD" (pages 85-93)

If you weren't thinking about yourself so much, maybe things wouldn't be so bad.

✓ From the chapter, what does this statement mean?

✓ How does it relate to your own life—to your past and your present?

✓ What changes does it lead you to consider?

You wake up, and right away, you think all about yourself—"me-me-me-me-meeeee!" You make all your plans, and when they fail throughout the day, when people say or do things you don't want,

262

now you're a pissed-off, miserable, unhappy person. Well, this isn't my world or yours. You only have a choice in how you receive this world, in how you respond. When you get let down, you have a bad day. How's that working for you? Instead, how about you take a step back and don't put so much expectation on everything? Then your feelings might not get hurt so much.

✓ From the chapter, what does this statement mean?

✓ How does it relate to your own life—to your past and your present?

✓ What changes does it lead you to consider?

***

"WHAT'S YOUR HEART SAYING YOU SHOULD DO?"
(pages 95-111)

The Mayo Clinic says spirituality "arises from your connection with yourself and with others, the development of your personal value system, and your search for meaning in life. For many, spirituality takes the form of religious observance, prayer, meditation or a belief in a higher power. For others, it can be found in nature, music, art or a secular community."[10]

[10] Mayo Foundation for Medical Education and Research. (2019, April 3). *Mayo mindfulness: Connecting spirituality and stress relief - mayo clinic news network.* Mayo Clinic. Retrieved February 26, 2023, from https://newsnetwork.mayoclinic.org/discussion/mayo-mindfulness-connecting-spirituality-and-stress-relief/. (Used with permission of Mayo Foundation for Medical Education and Research, all rights reserved.)

- What thoughts and feelings came up for you as you observed Rory's inner struggle between wanting to make his life better and feeling stuck in his addiction? How does shame contribute to the cycle of addiction? When have you experienced similar conflicts within yourself?

- Consider how you would define a "good person." What words or phrases would you include in your list? (The next time you find yourself on the verge of reacting, take a moment to pause and consider your list of values to guide what you say and do next.)

- Consider how Rory would define a "good life" and then create your own definition. Compile a list of activities that would bring you closer to this life. What current habits are a barrier?

- What relationships and communities in your life can help support you as you try to live out your values and vision of a good life? How can you intentionally deepen these connections?

***

"PULL BACK YOUR HOOD AND BE A PART OF. SAY YES."
(pages 113-124)

- Think about the people who have been mile markers of hope in your own life, who have shown faith and trust in you, despite your own doubts and past mistakes. How have they influenced your personal growth?

- What "head down" thinking were you recently stuck in where you were down on yourself?

- Identify a few specific "head up" experiences you've had in your life where you felt you mattered, like you had something to offer someone else. Look for trends. What do you want to do more of in your life?

- What are your go-to "head up" activities that you can engage in when you find yourself with your "head down"? Consider saying yes to a new experience that scares you a little (that won't cause harm) and ask yourself, "Whatcha got to lose?" You might just find yourself in an experience that lifts you.

***

"TRUST WE'RE ALL DOING THE BEST WE CAN WITH WHAT WE GOT AND WHAT WE KNOW" (pages 125-140)

Trust we're all doing the best we can with what we got and what we know.

✓ To what degree do you believe and practice this statement in your life? How might holding this belief affect how we relate to others?

✓ How might a reader who holds this belief view Rory's approach to parenting? How might a reader without this belief view Rory's approach to parenting?

✓ Choose two relationships from this chapter and examine to what extent they align with the statement above (for example, Rory's view of Alma or Sabina's view of herself).

***

"GOT A DREAM? GO! I'LL HOLD THE DOOR FOR YOU." AND "YOU CAN. I'LL SHOW YOU." (pages 141-172)

• What is the difference between a dream and a goal?

• How did Rory work toward his dreams, and what successes did he have? What setbacks did he encounter, and how did he meet them?

• What are your dreams? What setbacks do you foresee, and how can you meet them? What or who can help you stay motivated and keep going?

• Where do you see evidence of Rory's drive and determination in and out of addiction?

• Think back on your life: what are small and large moments that point to your drive and determination? (You can refer to these the next time you encounter a challenge that leaves you thinking, "I can't.") During conversations with others, pay attention to any signs that show a need for encouragement and support; you can help them recall past moments as evidence of just how capable they are.

"YOU BOPPING YOUR HEAD UP AND DOWN AGAIN? WHY DON'T YOU LOOK AT PEOPLE?" (pages 173-181)

- What's an example of a time you caught yourself "looking up" at others?

  ✓ What thoughts and feelings passed through you?

  ✓ Looking back on the event, what's revealed to you about yourself?

  ✓ How will you approach a similar situation next time?

- What's an example of a time you caught yourself "looking down" or "talking down" at others?

  ✓ What thoughts and feelings passed through you?

  ✓ Looking back on the event, what's revealed to you about yourself?

  ✓ How will you approach a similar situation next time?

- Consider a time when you felt a strong sense of connection with someone, where you looked them eye to eye and communicated authentically. How did that experience make you feel, and what impact did it have on your relationship? What can you do to stay level more often? What can you do to avoid becoming judgmental or distant from others?

- How does Rory's involvement in the recovery community shape his approach to others? How do you approach communication with or about individuals with addiction or homelessness? Are there any changes you would make?

***

"GOT A CHOICE TO MAKE? JUST PLAY THE STORY OUT." (pages 183-195)

- If you encountered someone who insists they don't have a choice when it comes to their addiction, how would you respond to them? Does Rory's perspective on choice in addiction resonate with you?

- Rory shares his personal struggle with the concept of the "gray area" in recovery. In your mind, is recovery an all-or-nothing approach, or do you believe there is room for moderation?

- Think about a decision you've been struggling to make. Play the whole story out from both ways:

  ✓ What would happen if you chose to keep things how they are?

  ✓ What would happen if you chose to make a change?

- "You are what you do, not what you did." How does this affirmation relate to your personal experiences?

"KEEP YOUR SIDE OF THE STREET CLEAN" (pages 197-205)

- Resentment often stems from past hurts and perceived wrongs. What insights from this chapter can help people overcome resentment and move toward forgiveness and healing?

- Consider a resentment you've been holding on to. How has it impacted your life? What would cleaning up the resentment look like so you can move on the best you can?

- Consider a time when you hurt someone through your words or actions, and the issue was never resolved. How has it impacted your life? What would cleaning up the mistake look like so you can move on the best you can?

- Describe how Rory faced the consequences of his actions and sought forgiveness. How did this impact his growth and healing?

***

"HOW WILL YOU SPEND THE TIME YOU'VE GOT LEFT?" (pages 207-222)

- What insights did you gain as you followed Rory's journey with cancer in this chapter?

- How did the diagnosis of aggressive cancer impact Rory's perspective on life and his priorities?

- Consider the quote: "Life is the space between the starting line—when you're born—and the finish line—when the curtain falls. Indian Mike taught me this way of thinking, to visualize it." Imagine your own timeline, take your age, and mark an "X." What do you want to start doing or do more of? What do you want to remove or do less of?

***

"LET THE GOOD THINGS YOU DO DEFINE YOU"
(pages 223-228)

- Given Rory's journey, why does he feel compelled to do good deeds and to help others?

- Consider what impact you hope to have on the world. How do you want to be remembered? What actions are you taking or plan to take to bring that vision to life?

REFERENCES

Common myths about addiction. Face It Together. (n.d.).
Retrieved February 26, 2023, from
https://www.wefaceittogether.org/learn/common-myths.
Mayo Clinic Staff (2022, October 4). *Drug addiction (substance use disorder).* Mayo Clinic. Retrieved February 26, 2023, from *https://www.mayoclinic.org/diseases-conditions/drug-addictions/symptoms-cause/syc-20365112.* (Used with permission of Mayo Foundation for Medical Education and Research, all rights reserved.)
Mayo Foundation for Medical Education and Research. (2019, April 3). *Mayo mindfulness: Connecting spirituality and stress relief - mayo clinic news network.* Mayo Clinic. Retrieved February 26, 2023, from *https://newsnetwork.mayoclinic.org/discussion/mayo-mindfulness-connecting-spirituality-and-stress-relief.* (Used with permission of Mayo Foundation for Medical Education and Research, all rights reserved.)

ACKNOWLEDGMENTS – S.P.

When I asked Tyler if he had a preference for a better pseudonym than "the hammock guy," he replied, "Go ahead and use my name. I live out loud now." Since then, I've thought about what "living out loud" entails: it means owning your past and how it's brought you to the place you are today. It means sharing the lessons you've learned along your journey—not as a prescription for others to follow, but as a source of empathy and hope.

The following people live out loud and granted me interviews. Thank you for sharing your connection to Rory and your personal stories:

Lilly. "You are what you do, not what you did."

Sabina. "I'm ready to stop fighting how I think my life should have gone. It went the only way it could."

Tim. "He's a mark on hundreds of people's hearts and lives. If you're in your darkest hour and thinking about giving up, Rory's a perfect example of why you shouldn't."

Jeremiah (Miah). "Stuck in traffic? It's a chance to practice patience for when you'll need it later. Rory taught me that."

Steve. "Every day since has been a bonus day."

Eric. "You can put ten people in front of someone saying the same thing, but if you're not able to emotionally connect with someone, no matter what you say or how you say it, it's not going to resonate."

Dale. "Rory practices what he preaches. That's what I call integrity."

Tyler. "When I was living homeless, words of encouragement meant the most to me because they gave me hope. And hope gave me the strength to pursue happiness again. You see, words are actions too."

Alma. "I'm discovering that if the right questions are asked, it's really easy to put down my memories into words." A reminder that every one of us has a story that's important to tell.

To Rory. Each time we meet, I'm left with new lines I want to add to the book so I always remember them. The experience of being immersed in this project has put me on a journey of living out loud. Maybe it's always a journey and never a destination. You've said all along that if our work can help even one person, that would be enough to justify all of our efforts. Well, I think I'm that one person. If anyone else connects with this book, it's a special bonus.

To Mom and Dad. Thank you for always encouraging me to pursue my passions. You both inspire me as I watch you continue to give your heart and dedication to your interests.

To my brother, Roshan. You were there for every phone call and video chat. I appreciate you being a sounding board from beginning to end of this project. Your advice was always spot-on.

To my mother-in-law, Renuka, and sister-in-law, Rupal. Thank you for sharing your stories. You're two of the strongest women I know.

To my kids, Kaiya and Kavi. I know I was at the computer an awful lot for two years. You would remind me about the dangers of too much screen time. Yet you stayed patient…especially when dinner was brinner once again that week.

And to my husband, Chirag. Only you and I know what a life-changer this book has been. I couldn't have written it without your belief in me and all the meals you cooked so I wouldn't lose momentum.

To the superintendent, Dr. Kent Pekel, and the sabbatical committee. This book wouldn't exist without the dedicated time needed to record Rory's story and piece together his journey and mine. Thank you for seeing something in my fragmented vision for this book and taking a chance on us.

To all of my friends and family. Thank you for excitedly asking about the progress of my book and how you couldn't wait to read it. It put a good kind of pressure on me and meant the work I was doing mattered.

To the Burn Boot Camp community. Leyton and Trayton, thank you for being a voice in my ear when I needed a mental push to see this project through. Your message—*You can do hard things*—was a much needed reminder on days when I was paralyzed with self-doubt. To my fellow Burn members. Seeing you show up every day helped me stay disciplined in my writing, even when I wasn't always feeling it.

To the pickleball community. Thank you for being there when I needed a break and for always being so welcoming and taking a moment to connect.

To my beta readers. A huge thank-you for your time and willingness to read an unpolished manuscript. Heather Willman, Marian Holtorf, Alexis Zaccariello, Sabina Londer, Lilly Londer,

Jay Wangen, Leah Baethke, Katie Sloan, Inga Rogers, and Julie Ruzek: I took all of your notes to heart to help Rory's messages come through to the reader on the other side. The book is better for it. I owe you one.

To my book's helpers. Carmen, you're one hell of an editor. Thank you for embracing this book and guiding this first-time author with empathy (especially with the necessary yet heart-wrenching cuts). David, you created a cover image that so beautifully captures Rory's lonely world with a glimpse of hope just beyond. I'm grateful our paths crossed. Anna, I was lucky to have your incredible editor's eye for detail in the final stages of this book. And Erin, thank you for making us feel at ease during the photo shoot.

To the staff at the Rochester ALC. I've appreciated your support over the years for every crazy idea I've come to you with to try. Thank you for not throwing any tomatoes! Seriously, the way you love and care for our students—even when they test us—inspires me. I've grown as a teacher within this team of encouraging, creative, and dedicated professionals. A special shout-out to Steven, licensed drug/alcohol counselor, for helping students in their journey to recovery.

Finally, to our students: when I'm lucky enough to be a part of your inner circle and to learn your stories, I'm left in awe of your resilience. I hope this book reminds you of the strength within you and keeps you on a path toward your goals in life. Live with your hood pulled back—engage with the world—because you have so much to give.

ACKNOWLEDGMENTS – R.L.

Sweta, this book would not have happened without you. Your tenacity is what brought us here. I am grateful to the Rochester school district for granting you a sabbatical. Thank you for trusting in me and never giving up even through the time I was sick and unreachable. You really know me better than I know myself at times. I love you.

In my sobriety, I have built a found family. I could never have come this far without all of the people, halfway houses, treatment centers, shelters, and recovery groups I've met on my journey. They have made me who I am. I do the most learning in life when things are hard and I hurt. For many of us in recovery, we spend those times of hurt together. Cody, we have been there for each other in some of the worst times of our lives. I am grateful to have a friend to weather those experiences with.

Dale, thank you for sharing your journey to make amends with your family. I will always cherish that beautiful day.

Eric, seeing you grow from the man you once were into the man, father, and professional you are today is nothing short of miraculous. Thank you for helping me believe in miracles.

Steve, I am so proud of the choices you have made to become the man you have become. I love you, buddy. Keep that necklace close.

Miah, I love you. Today I got a dollar, and so do you. Look how far we've come.

To the new owners of Rory's Home Improvement (Jesse, Heidi, and the team), thank you for carrying on Rory's Home Improvement with integrity and respect. I love you guys.

To my godchildren, Makana and Landon, what a gift you are, and what gratitude I have that your parents trust me enough to hold this honor. You have been a light for me on my worst days.

I also want to give thanks to my "blood family" for their willingness to share pieces of our family's story and be a part of this experience with me.

To my wife, Lilly. From the moment I met you, I knew I wanted to spend the rest of my life with you. Not a day has gone by that has been dull or boring. Your parents, Paul and Nancy, have shown me acceptance and kindness since the first time I met them, for that I am grateful. Thank you for loving me exactly the way that I am and never leaving my side. I love you, baby.

Sabina, I seem to repeat throughout the story, "I didn't know what I wanted, but I knew it wasn't this." In that hotel room, as I looked at that picture of three-year-old you, I was sure I knew what I wanted for the first time: to be your father. I truly don't believe I would be here today if it wasn't for you. Thank you for continuing to love me unconditionally and being willing to share me with everyone all these years.

To Tim and his children, I am so grateful to be a part of your lives now. The trips we've been able to take together have been so meaningful.

To my eldest brother, I love you.

To my parents, how I wish we had had more time together. Though our time was short, I learned so much from each of you that has helped me survive. Your contrasting personalities taught me how to find balance.

To all of those I have lost, may you be at peace and know not a day goes by that I don't think of you. I love you all.

To the Mayo Clinic. Life had been going so well till I found myself alone in a hospital room in the middle of the COVID crisis. I thought I had learned what fear was in addiction, but fear can come in many forms. All it takes is one moment of one day and your whole life changes. In my eyes, the Mayo Clinic is the best hospital in the world. Thank you for taking such good care of me through one of the most medically challenging times of my life. Your care and compassion have left an unforgettable impact on me and my family.

To the Ronald McDonald House, thank you for allowing me to be a part of your amazing organization. It was brief, but I found a sense of worth for the first time in a long time at that point of my journey.

To the community of Rochester, you have given me a life I could never have dreamed of. The people gave me a chance to become a productive member of this community. That chance was all I needed to prosper. I promise to keep building up the community that built me. Thank you.

Thank you to all the students at the ALC who I have had the opportunity to meet over the years, and for your letters too. I believe everything happens for a reason and I meet people when the time is right. You are what keeps me coming back, with my two feet on the ground. I see you.

TO OUR READERS

Spreading this message of connection and belonging is so important to us. If this book helped you, moved you, or simply entertained you, please take a moment to post a rating or review so others can find it too. That goes a long way toward giving others the gift of hope.

Visit us at www.shouldvebeendead.com.

Made in the USA
Monee, IL
30 April 2024

57724178R00162